Readability

The advisory editor to the series is
John E. Merritt, Professor of Educational Studies,
The Open University, Milton Keynes.

Readability
John Gilliland

HODDER AND STOUGHTON
London   Sydney   Auckland   Toronto
for the United Kingdom Reading Association

Acknowledgments

It is a truism that a book is the work of many people, and I would like to thank the many friends and colleagues with whom readability has been discussed. I owe particular thanks to John Merritt, for his helpful criticism and encouragement, Michael Bamlett, for his help in preparing the index and references, and Vera Crosby for her help in the production of the manuscript. Lastly, I am especially grateful to my wife, Marian, whose typing skills, patience and understanding I have so heavily drawn upon.

John Gilliland

ISBN 0 340 15017 3

Printed and bound in Great Britain for
Hodder and Stoughton Educational,
a division of Hodder and Stoughton Ltd, London,
by Unwin Brothers Limited,
The Gresham Press, Old Woking, Surrey

Contents

Preface

So many books are being published in the education field today
that it is very difficult for teachers to keep in touch with research
and new developments. This series of monographs has been
devised both to collate new ideas and to save teachers of reading
from having to spend much of their valuable time searching out
relevant texts and materials.

Each monograph will deal with a specific problem area (for
example, modern innovations in teaching reading, reading
readiness, the development of fluency, problems of assessment),
giving a review of theoretical considerations and published
research, and pointing out their important practical implications.

Professor J. E. Merritt
Department of Educational Studies
The Open University, Milton Keynes

Part 1 **Introduction**

Chapter 1 General Background

When reading for information, a reader usually intends to extract what he wants from the text, and not merely to absorb what the author presents. For his part, an author, when intent upon transmitting information, must firstly help the reader to perceive the relationship between his own particular information needs and the content and major issues to be dealt with in the book. The initial part of any exposition, therefore, should answer the question, 'What is it all about?' and 'How are these ideas organised so that the various relationships between the different ideas can be readily understood?' In the case of this book, these two questions will be tackled by means of an examination of the concept of readability, and the practical ways in which it has been investigated.

The second responsibility of the author is to help the reader by indicating important theoretical and practical applications for the material presented. In the case of this book, it is important to show exactly how an understanding of readability can lead, directly or indirectly, to improvement in the preparation or selection of reading materials so that they are neither too easy nor too difficult for the readership concerned. An indication of the kinds of people who would find this sort of knowledge valuable, and when and how it might be applied is, therefore, the second topic to be covered in this chapter.

The author has a third responsibility, and that is to help the reader to gain a broad perspective so that he can judge the importance of the immediately relevant material. This may be done by providing an historical context and this is the third topic to be covered in this chapter. An adequate context, however, must also entail a discussion of the whole field of reading. In this book, it is only possible to give a brief indication of the relevance of readability to broader issues in the field of reading. The reader can study these broader issues in more detail by referring to the other monographs in this series.

A fourth indication is that he should show clearly how the book itself is organised in relation to the topic. The structure of a theoretical framework does not necessarily provide the best framework for presenting a readable exposition. The fourth topic in this chapter, therefore, will be the organisation of the book itself.

This first part of the book can be seen to involve four questions, each of which will be considered in turn:

1 What is meant by the word readability?
2 Who might find information about readability useful?
3 What is the previous history of readability?
4 What is the purpose of the remainder of the book?

1 WHAT IS READABILITY?

Readability is primarily concerned with a basic problem familiar to all people who choose books for their own use, or who choose books for others to use. This is a problem of matching. On the one hand there is a collection of individuals with given interests and reading skills. On the other hand, there is a range of books and other reading materials, differing widely in content, style and complexity. The extent to which the books can be read with profit will be determined largely by the way in which the two sides are matched. For example, a person who is a competent reader may soon be deterred from reading if his choice is restricted to simple repetitive texts. Similarly, a person with limited reading ability will soon become discouraged if he is given texts which are beyond his comprehension.

In choosing books for himself, the reader will be influenced not only by his range of interests but also by the way in which the books have been written. For example, books which look 'wordy' or complicated may be avoided even though the content and style might be acceptable on closer examination. Of course, many people other than the reader himself are also involved in this matching exercise.

The study of this problem of matching reader and text has come to be called 'readability'. There is always a danger of coining new words unnecessarily. However, it is hoped that as the topic is developed further, it will become apparent that the term is not only a convenient label to describe a particular kind of study, but refers to a clearly definable concept, which has many applications.

Most readers will be able to make an intelligent guess as to how 'readability' might be defined. It has to do with the interest or the ease with which a book can be read. However, during the course of time casual definitions have had to be sharpened and a number of considered and detailed alternatives have been proposed. An example of such a definition is that of Dale and Chall (1948) which states that:

'In the broadest sense, readability is the sum total (including interactions) of all those elements within a given piece of printed material that affects the success which a group of readers have with it. The success is the extent to which they understand it, read it at optimum speed and find it interesting.'

This definition stresses three aspects of the reading process: c omprehension, fluency, and interest. Reading comprehension is usually thought of as being concerned only with the meaning which we can attach to the print, but it is of course dependent upon fluency and interest.

The main emphasis in this definition is upon the elements which lead to comprehension, that is, upon the understanding of words, and phrases, and the relating of ideas in the passage to our experience. The second factor, fluency, is the extent to which a person can read a given text at optimum speed. This element of the definition lays emphasis on the perceptual aspects of reading. It reflects such aspects of reading as the ease with which the text may be seen and the ease with which letters and words can be identified. These factors relate to primary reading skills which a reader must have already acquired if he is to comprehend what he reads. It also refers to the relationship between the linguistic skill of the reader and the syntactic complexity of the text. The third component of the Dale and Chall definition refers to the motivational factors which will affect interest. Although this aspect of the definition is placed third, interest and motivation play a critical part in determining readability.

As Dale and Chall point out, these three elements of the definition are not separate. They interact with each other to affect readability. The importance of these interaction effects may readily be appreciated. For example, in a scientific article, complex technical terms may be necessary to describe certain concepts. A knowledge of the subject will make it easier for a reader to cope with these terms and they, in turn, may help him to sort out his ideas, thus making the text more readable. This interaction between vocabulary and content will affect the extent to which some people can read the text with ease. Similarly, some uncommon words and ideas may be familiar to some readers because of their experience and interests. If the text itself is difficult because of the ways in which the ideas are expressed, then interaction between vocabulary and reader's knowledge will affect readability.

The three factors isolated in this definition and the additional effects of interaction are a source of confusion and misunderstanding in many studies of readability. The three factors are very different and bear little relationship to one another. Yet they have still been collected together and treated as equal in a single statement. Similarly, interactions are referred to but not isolated and considered separately. Therefore, when we look at measures which are supposed to reflect this definition of readability, some short-comings are immediately obvious. For example, the measures which we encounter often involve only one of the elements in the definition. This creates a problem in that the results of different readability measures may not be freely compared.

Other definitions of readability do not embody the same factors as those included in the Dale and Chall definition. For example, English and English (1958) define readability as 'the quality of a written or printed communication that makes it easy for a given class of persons to understand its meaning or that induces them to continue reading'. As may be seen, in this case persistence at reading has been combined with comprehension to provide two principal factors in readability. While such a definition is acceptable, it does not draw attention to all the components of readability and so is rather less useful than the Dale and Chall definition. On the other hand, its emphasis on the text and its properties, rather than the reader, draw our attention to the fact that we must analyse text and reader separately, as well as in combination.

McLaughlin (1968) argues that readability is best defined as 'the degree to which a given class of people find certain reading matter compelling and, necessarily, comprehensible.' This definition emphasises characteristics of the reader as well as the degree of 'compellingness' of the text. McLaughlin regards this latter as a necessary factor since compellingness and comprehension are so closely related. He argues that a definition of readability must be based on the characteristics of the readers, as it can be assumed that people will tend to continue to read only that which they understand. McLaughlin argues further that a classification of texts which have been chosen by readers will provide a more satisfactory basis for the construction of measures of readability than texts selected at random from the range available, since a selection on the former basis will reflect the degree of interest shown by particular groups of readers.

2 WHO MIGHT FIND READABILITY STUDIES HELPFUL?

Given that the subject matter of readability studies is the matching of readers and books, it will be evident that the subject should be of interest and valuable to a variety of people, not only those in professional situations.

Firstly, the study of readability will, or should, be of immediate concern to writers. For example, in the area of non-fiction, the intention of the author is to communicate expressly facts, theories, impressions, attitudes and values. His ability to do this may be considerably influenced by the knowledge which he has of the reading ability of his potential readers, and by this knowledge of the way in which such things as sentence construction and the arrangement of ideas can influence understanding. Measures of readability offer him a means of testing, quickly and reliably, the efficiency of his communication. For the teacher seeking to write for children the study of readability might be of particular benefit since it provides a systematic basis on which to judge the appropriateness of reading material for children of various abilities.

Next, from the point of view of the consumer, readability measures could provide information about the relative difficulty of texts which, when applied, could save readers time and effort. Teachers, in particular, are faced with an ever increasing flood of printed materials which differ widely in content, style and difficulty, and from which selections have to be made. In this situation, readability studies may help by providing the teacher with an additional guide to help him both to select and to organise material suitable for particular children. This means of sorting reading material would be particularly useful in assessing books for use by children on projects, or, in general, where supervision of the children's own selections is not always possible. A further advantage to the teacher lies, as we shall see later, in the possibility of adapting some methods of studying readability for use as teaching techniques, thus enabling children to improve their skill in reading and comprehension.

Librarians, like teachers, are a professional group who are involved in the process of selecting and organising reading materials for use by others. They already provide readers, children and adults alike, with general information about the content of books by means of various classificatory systems. However, librarians could further assist the readers by giving them some broad indication of the relative difficulty of the range of books which is available. If such information could be given, in the form of a colour code, for example, then readers could perhaps be saved a great deal of time and effort and frustration. The study of readability would seem, then, to offer to various consumers, readers, teachers and librarians, the possibility of meeting the age old exhortation to ensure that the right book reaches the hands of the right person at the right time.

Publishers also might profit from a knowledge of the results of readability studies. In the preparation of texts for students of all

15

ages, the control of the level of reading difficulty will make a series more attractive to buyers, particularly if the details of the studies undertaken prior to publication are made available to the potential users of the books so that they can judge how well the material is likely to cater for the abilities of different groups of children.

3 HISTORICAL PERSPECTIVE

Although the definitions mentioned above are relatively recent, and refer to communication in print, there is evidence of a long and sustained interest in the assessment of the effectiveness of the spoken word. Advocates of the need for clear speech have quoted St Paul (1 Corinthians 14:9).

'Except ye utter by the tongue words easy to be understood how shall it be known what is spoken?'

Lorge (1944) explains how the Talmudists, in compiling and studying the body of laws called the Talmud, counted the occurrences of words and ideas in seeking to distinguish differences in meaning. It is not surprising that evidence of an interest in clear speech and readability should come from religious writings. Religious sects and orders were the most literate and, in many cases, the only literate persons in the communities. In addition, they were of necessity very much concerned with the communication of ideas. Just as the need for effective communication was recognised by speakers, so the desirability of ensuring a close match between the reader and books by various forms of systematic assessment has been recognised for some time.

It is not surprising then that educators in general should show an interest in readability. Klare (1963), for example, reports cases of individual educationists in the nineteenth century who related counts of vocabulary and familiar words to reading difficulty. The results of these investigations represent the first attempts to appraise the difficulty of texts objectively.

From the beginning of this century, the study of readability has been concerned with the search for factors in the text which could be easily counted and incorporated into measures which are objective. These measures usually took the form of a formula, and the procedures often involved lengthy calculations. Unfortunately, the word 'formula' itself has also frequently acted as a deterrent to many people who might have gained from the use of the formulae devised. Formulae which have provided the most common measures of readability have shown certain stages of development which reflect the aims and intentions of the designers and also changes in the demands of the people using the formulae.

16

Klare describes the chronological sequence in the growth of these formulae and outlines four main stages.

An early series of formulae were produced between 1920 and 1934 (see Klare 1963, Chapter 4). Though crude and clumsy in operation, they did in fact use aspects of the texts, such as vocabulary range, and the number of prepositions or polysyllabic words, which were refined to produce reliable measures of readability. These early formulae were applied generally and gave only approximate ratings of the difficulty of the texts. In the period from 1934–1938, the formulae devised tended to become more detailed and reflected a concern for greater accuracy and reliability. These measures involved the use of aspects of the text, but required the laborious collection of statistics as well as lengthy calculations.

The detailed formulae of this period were soon superceded by a series of formulae in which efficiency and simplicity of use were the prime considerations. This change of emphasis reflected the practical requirements of the teachers and other workers who were using the formulae in situations where the time and effort which could be given were strictly limited. Klare suggests that this period extended from 1938 until 1953.

The latest period in the development of formulae, reported by Klare, extends from 1953 until 1959 and shows a shift of emphasis on to the development of specialised formulae for particular purposes. These specialised formulae were devised to deal with the characteristics of particular kinds of reading material, such as children's readers, or with particular readability factors such as the level of abstractness in a passage.

More recently, interest in readability has revived as a result of an increase in the volume and variety of forms of printed material and the increasingly strong demand for universal literacy. This has led to an increase in the need to search yet further for accurate measures for predicting and controlling the difficulty of texts. The possibility of using new methods of measurement such as charts and sentence completion precedures which vary from the traditional approach has assisted in this revival. Also, recent studies in linguistics have added to our understanding of language and the part which it plays in reading. This understanding has permitted a more coherent and theoretically supported approach to the practical problems involved in measuring readability.

4 THE REMAINDER OF THE MONOGRAPH

From this brief coverage of background information, it can be seen that 'readability' is not simply an unnecessary new word, which does not refer to anything in particular. It does, in fact, describe a clearly defined concept. In addition, it can be seen that techniques used to study the problem and also the evidence which has been produced may be of use to a number of different people in different professions, all of whom however are concerned with the effectiveness of communication through reading. The further development of this study now involves a more detailed discussion of two principal questions.

Firstly, what factors can we find which interact to determine how readable a person finds a book? This, of course, needs to be followed by a subsidiary question. How may these factors be controlled and altered to increase the effectiveness of reading? These factors are dealt with in Part 2 of the monograph.

Secondly, how may we measure readability and so increase the effectiveness of our attempts to match reader and print? Again, how may this be done with maximum convenience and efficiency by those who need this kind of information? It will be seen that Part 3 of the monograph is concerned with this aspect of the study.

Since the reader may wish to follow up particular findings and perhaps put into practice some of the suggestions in the work, the annotated bibliography gives brief details of the books listed so that their suitability for further reading can be more accurately judged. This bibliography is small and the references included have been selected in terms of the practical activities which they suggest as well as their suitability for further reading on the subject of readability.

Part 2   Readers and Books

Chapter 2 Interest and Motivation

The first and foremost consideration in the assessment of readability is the reader. There is always a danger when talking of 'the reader', that we may forget that we are, in fact, considering individuals who show wide differences in their attitudes towards reading and in the amount of time they devote to it. While the importance of individual differences is recognised, it is nevertheless necessary to seek out and describe in general terms, factors which will affect all readers, to a greater or lesser extent, when they tackle the printed word.

We can list a large variety of physical and mental characteristics of the reader which may have temporary or prolonged effects upon his reading ability and hence the readability of the texts he chooses. In this part of the monograph, the main factors will be dealt with under three headings.

The initial factor in a person which affects his reading is the degree of interest which he shows in it. Motivational influences affect the choice of books and interest, in turn, may be affected by the format of a book. This chapter, therefore, deals with the relationship between interest motivation, and the selection of books. A second basic relationship affecting readability is that between the reader's perceptual skill and the printed characters which he has to see and read. Studies involving the visibility of print are referred to in Chapter 3.

The third factor which affects the way in which a person reads is language. The importance of language as a major influence in reading has long been recognised and it is natural that this should be reflected in the amount of space devoted to it here. Also, as will be seen, many of the linguistic factors described have been used in the measurement of readability. For these reasons Chapters 4, 5, 6 and 7 all deal with various aspects of language and their effect upon readability. As the table of contents indicates, language has been classified and analysed in units of different size ranging from small units, i.e. sounds, to large units, i.e. paragraphs, each of which have different characteristics. Each is referred to in a separate section.

We all know, from our own experiences, how much easier it is to apply ourselves to something we like doing, and how much more we learn when we are interested than when the task is a chore. Happily, many teachers recognise this fact and, whenever possible, exploit the existing interests of the children. Further learning and understanding is also encouraged by the stimulation of new interests and enthusiasms.

Teachers of young children are well aware of the effect which a lively interest in looking at and talking about books can have on a child's progresss in learning to read. It is equally important, of course, to maintain this interest once the child is fluent and reading independently, since an individual's basis for judging the readability of a text will be largely determined by whether he thinks it will interest him. Interest and motivation provide a good starting point since they are important to the study of readability and they may be influenced to some extent by the teacher.

1 INTEREST AND MOTIVATION

The degree of motivation which readers show towards books will depend upon the nature and quality of interest, the sources of the interest and motivation, and variations in focus of interest.

a The nature of interests

When we talk about a book being interesting we are often referring to the enjoyment which it gives us or to the extent to which it arouses pleasurable feelings. This essentially emotional reaction, called an affective response, may reflect either stable long standing aspects of the individual's personality, or temporary emotional states. In either case, the effect upon our interest is very strong and it plays a significant part in determining not only the subjects chosen but also our tolerance of difficulties in the text. We can use the term 'responsive reading' (c.f. Morris 1963) when interest is based primarily upon an affective response.

Alternatively, we may talk about a book being 'interesting' because of the intellectual stimulus which it provides or because of the way in which it assists in solving problems. Interests with this cognitive basis may reflect pervasive elements in the individual's character, such as curiosity, or perhaps problems which can most conveniently be solved by reference to books. Here, we are concerned primarily with reading for information. Needless to say, we may obtain a lot of information when we are indulging in responsive reading just as we may get a lot of emotional satisfaction when we are reading for information.

Nevertheless, our actual selection of material, ranging from say comics to car manuals, is determined by the nature of our primary interest, affective or cognitive: for example, the comic will usually be picked up for pleasure, although it may happen also to satisfy intellectual curiosity. The car manual may be read primarily for enjoyment by a car enthusiast, but he will also, of course, acquire a lot of information. On the other hand, another individual may read it solely in order to determine why his car does not start, i.e. for information.

b Sources of interest and motivation

The most powerful factors influencing interest are those which come from within, whether they be cognitive or affective. These internal or intrinsic factors provide a strong motivation to read. For example, a person may devote years to reading in order to satisfy his personal curiosity or, perhaps, to prove to himself that he is capable of reading about and understanding a particular kind of subject. Such intrinsic factors may lead, in some cases, to the reading of extremely complex and varied material. On the other hand, however, they may lead to the restriction of reading to a narrow band of similar texts, as in the case of the reader who always seeks the same kind of detective novel.

From this discussion of interest, we can easily see how these influences will affect our approach to a text. For example, we may be so highly motivated that we read print well above the level of difficulty to which we are accustomed. Subsequently, the sense of achievement in reading may itself become an important factor in stimulating interest—an added bonus of which the experienced teacher is well aware, and always seeks to exploit.

The interest which we display towards a book is also influenced by external factors. These external, or extrinsic factors, can often be manipulated to encourage learning and persistence at a task. Teachers use a variety of techniques to maintain interest. Teacher approval, by bringing pleasure, may lead the child to show and maintain interest in reading, in the absence of intrinsic influences. More tangible rewards, such as marks or stars, have been used. Examinations and job requirements will also affect the sort of reading and the level at which it is undertaken. Unfortunately, the desire to gain stars or succeed in examinations may act as an incentive even though little pleasure is gained from the reading. In this case, the reader is not behaving out of 'interest' but from compulsion. Having opted, for example, to take an examination voluntarily, he is compelled to read at certain levels in order to ensure success. The level of difficulty of a passage may turn out to be so high as to deter him from attempting to master it, even though, with strong intrinsic motivation he might have been capable of dealing with it. It is impossible in practice to predict the way in which a wide variety of influences, such as those quoted above, will affect the performance of a given individual. In spite of the many difficulties, however, the importance of these influences has been recognised and has not been neglected in studies of readability.

Klare (1963) examined the influence upon readability scores of a motivational state described as a 'set to learn', that is, a disposition or attitude towards a task and which affects our performance of the task. Differences in scores obtained by students on recall tests after reading a series of short technical passages were noted and related to the existence of a strong or weak 'set to learn'. A weak 'set to learn' was characterised by the adoption of a mechanical or habitual approach to the reading task, whereas a strong 'set to learn' was characterised by a more deliberate attack with a more regular eye fixation pattern and different speed of reading. Klare found that the easier passages were read more quickly whether a strong or weak set was adopted but that comprehension (recall score) of the more readable passages was higher only where a strong 'set to learn' existed. This effect of a 'set to learn' helps to account for the findings in some readability studies in which increasing readability consistently produced faster reading but only occasionally greater comprehension scores. This 'set to learn' is a reflection of a motivational state and it is clear from this investigation that some measures of readability using comprehension scores reflect the motivational state of the readers but measures involving speed of reading are less likely to do so.

A further reflection of the motivational state of the reader, which is a general factor in human behaviour, but which affects reading performance, is the 'principle of least effort' expounded by Zipf (1949), and noted by Thorndike. This principle states that a person minimises the amount of effort necessary to obtain a certain goal. Klare (1963) found that preferences for reading material were governed by the simplicity of the text, and that college students could make accurate choices as to which texts would be easier to read. He also reported that the students generally read more of simpler texts than of those which are harder. It is well established that material chosen to be read for pleasure is usually very much simpler than that which a person would normally be capable of reading. The 'set to learn' must be strong or the goal important if the individual is to raise his performance in reading by a significant amount.

The operation of motivational influences poses a problem for the researcher wishing to measure the readability of print. If the choice of material is left to the reader, then the performance measured will generally be below that which the reader could achieve. If material is chosen by the researcher, the presence of a strong or weak 'set to learn' can affect considerably the scores obtained and, as a result, render the measure of the passage unreliable. From the teacher's point of view, a readability measure is required which can be used to assess the level at which a reader is reading for choice and also the extent to which his level of performance can be raised by the presence of a strong 'set to learn'.

c Variations in focus of interest

Many variations in interest can be accounted for by the nature of interest and the source of interest described earlier. Further variations, however, are encountered when we examine the effects of personal characteristics, such as experience and age, upon interests in reading.

The experiences which an individual has had will obviously affect his interests. Teachers recognise the need to broaden a child's experiences since these provide the basis for the growth and understanding of language. In addition, the effect which exposure to books at home and in school can have upon interest in reading and reading progress is also well known and influences the choice of reading materials. For example, reading materials prepared for use in compensatory educational projects stress the 'interest value' for children.

Experienced teachers and librarians are well aware that the kinds of books preferred will be affected by the age, sex, experience and intelligence of the reader. Chall (1958) collected evidence from various sources and reached some helpful, though easily anticipated, conclusions. Wide variations in reading interest were reported in both sexes and in different age ranges, though some fairly consistent themes were to be found. For example, children between the ages of six to eight were found to be interested in stories of animals, children, familiar experiences, nature and fairies, and stories involving surprise and humour. No significant difference in preference between the sexes was reported. Between the ages of eight to twelve boys showed a prevalent interest in action, mystery, sport and realistic animal stories. Girls, on the other hand, showed an interest in stories of home and school life. Boys and girls showed a common interest in action and humour. Beyond the age of twelve adventure and humour interested both boys and girls, whilst girls also showed an interest in love stories.

2 INFLUENCE ON ENJOYMENT AND UNDERSTANDING

It has already been established that the interest of the reader will play a significant part in determining how he reads a book. This interest was seen to depend upon how he feels at the time, what he needs to know and the influence of his previous experiences. In addition, however, factors in the book have been found to influence the extent to which a reader enjoys and understands what he reads.

From a casual observation of adults or children selecting their own books, we can soon see that several aesthetic factors first draw attention to a particular choice. The size of the book, the design of the cover, the illustrations and even the 'feel' of pages can arouse interest and spur the individual into selecting one book rather than another.

Once a person has begun to look at the print other considerations begin to affect the degree to which he will persist. Chall (1958) reports a series of studies in which the influence of format, content, style, etcetera were considered. She quotes a survey by Gray and Leary (1935) in which the content of the book was found to be the most important factor, with style of writing, format and organisation also affecting interest in decreasing order of importance. The readers' opinions concerning the effect of these factors upon readability were found to agree generally with the opinions of librarians, teachers and publishers.

Chall reports another study, by Strang, in which high school and college students were asked to list factors which they thought made books readable. Stylistic factors such as 'plain everyday English' or 'easy simple vocabulary' and 'short paragraphs and sentences' were found to be most common. Content was placed second, with frequent references to such aspects as action, suspense, and modern characters. Format was ranked third with students preferring 'not too many pages', 'not too many chapters', and organisation was ranked last.

Chall also reports a study by Engelmans in which children were found to prefer a conversational style of writing to a narrative expository style. The format was found to be read more quickly when speed of reading tests were given. More recently, in a report published in this country, Clarke (1970) briefly described a series of factors, including design and colour, which a group of teachers regarded as suitable criteria to use in judging the suitabliity of reading material, particularly for disadvantaged children. Although based on subjective judgements, the conclusions do reflect the importance which format and production are thought to play in provoking interest in a book.

The findings of such studies are useful in providing general bases on which to judge the readability of books. However, the subjectivity of interest and the lack of direct control over it reduces the usefulness of these conclusions for teachers and it is to more precisely measurable aspects of books that attention must be directed.

Information of this kind does not permit the teacher to make an accurate prediction about the readability of a text in respect of a particular individual. It does, however, clarify, or at least confirm, his judgement about the range of interests to be catered for, in the case of groups of children of a particular age, ability level or sex.

Chapter 3　The Visibility of Print

We have examined some aspects of the reader which affect his performance in reading. We now turn to a particular aspect of the book which influences the reader's performance and that is, the print. A person cannot find a book readable if he cannot see the printed characters on a page. It is clear that, before any significance can be attached to single letters or sequences of letters and words, they have to be perceived and recognised. Factors which influence the ease with which we see print are usually described in the literature, under the heading of either visibility or legibility.

This chapter then is concerned with the visual perception of letter shapes, isolated words and words in context, and those factors of type construction and setting, which affect the ability to identify letters and words, and therefore fluency. The purpose of the chapter is also to establish the extent to which it may be possible to produce ideal or 'optimum' conditions for legibility and to indicate, by reference to previous studies, what those conditions might be. Whilst these factors have been studied using fluent readers as subjects, studies in legibility will also be seen to be relevant to children learning to read.

First, a caution: Tinker (1963) describes a variety of methods which have been employed in studies of legibility. As a result the term legibility has been defined differently in different contexts and so results must be interpreted carefully when they are related to readability. Tinker (1963) lists the advantages and disadvantages of the various methods used to date in *Legibility of Print*, chapter 2. The two general methods described are referred to as threshold measures and rate measures.

Threshold techniques measure the accuracy with which letters or words are perceived when they are seen for only limited periods of time, or at varying distances. By altering the time of exposure of the print, after a series of trials, the experimenter finds a critical exposure speed. If examples of print are exposed at speeds slower than this, then the print can be identified accurately. On the other hand, if the items are exposed at speeds faster than the critical speed, they cannot be identified accurately. By measuring differences in the exposure times at which different kinds of print are perceived, it is possible to establish which is more legible. Similarly, by measuring differences in distance at which letters or words are correctly identified, the legibility or visibility of print can be determined. The results of this type of study are helpful in the redesigning and improvement of print. These measures are less useful however in studying the effect of such factors as optimum type size in continuous text. The reason for this is that only small items can be presented at one time, and the measures involve the use of complicated laboratory procedures.

Rate measures used to assess legibility involve such methods as the rate of work, i.e. the amount of material read in a given time, the average number of eye blinks per minute, or the speed and accuracy of reading performance. Differences in the legibility of texts are reflected in the different rates measures. For example, a less legible text is found to cause more eye blinks per minute and to produce a greater number of inaccuracies in reading than a more legible one. These measures are applied when the reader is dealing with continuous text and closely reflect ease of reading or fluency. For these reasons, they are more relevant to readability than threshold measures. On the other hand, though these measures relate to one aspect of readability, it must be recognised that this is only a minor aspect, and that rate measures do not offer a means of assessing more general aspects of readability.

Bearing in mind the advantages and disadvantages of each kind of measure, let us now consider the various aspects of legibility in turn.

1 LEGIBILITY OF LETTERS AND DIGITS

Various reports demonstrate noticeable variations in the legibility of letters of the alphabet when printed in upper and lower case. Tinker (1963) summarised these reports with suggestions for improving the legibility of 'poor visibility' letters in lower case. His general findings were as follows:

letters of high legibility   d m p q w
letters of medium legibility   j r v x y
letters of low legibility   c e i n l

Most of the studies referred to by Tinker were based on the perception of isolated letters and material with little contextual meaning. M. D. Vernon (1929), however, has shown that confusion of similarly shaped letters does not occur in the normal reading of comprehensible material. Confusion was found to occur when the material had little contextual meaning.

If this is so, then poor legibility of letters may not be a significant factor for fluent readers but may be an impediment to children learning to read. This might be particularly important when discriminations of the following types of words are to be made with poor contextual clues: 'horse' and 'house', 'come' and 'came', 'white' and 'while'. Certainly, Shaw's (1969) findings in a study of partially sighted adults and children support the conclusion that print requirements may be critical for beginning readers. Spencer (1969) also reports a series of studies which produced similar conclusions.

These findings suggest that the differentiation of the easily confused letters might be assisted by careful variation of the following factors (examples of different type faces are given in table 1, page 31):

a serifs
b heaviness of stroke
c emphasis of distinguishing characteristics
d simplification of outline
e emphasis of white space inside the letter
f width of letter.

On the other hand aesthetic, economic and technical considerations may well lead to a low value being placed upon legibility. In fact, regrettable though this may be, tradition and convention may play a greater part than the results of legibility studies in the selection of print for texts. Here, then, is an area in which the teacher, acting through his professional associations might well influence and improve the quality and suitability of the type faces which children encounter.

2 TYPE AND TYPE FORMS

There are numerous designs of type faces. Williamson (1966), for example, lists 76 type faces which are at present available and used by British printers. Although these type faces show wide variations in appearance (see examples below), there are some characteristics which are common to many. For example, several different faces make use of short finishing strokes or *serifs* at the top and bottom of a letter. Designs which do not carry these strokes are called *sans serif* types. Most books are set with serif type faces but sans serif is sometimes used for school books, particularly readers for young children. Those type faces in which strokes have been thickened are referred to as *bold* face.

Many studies of the legibility of these different type faces have

Table 1: Examples of type faces in current use (this book is set in Roman)

9 pt roman	9 pt italic	9 pt bold
CASLON (serif)		
the brown fox jumps	*the brown fox jumps*	
PLANTIN (serif)		
the brown fox jumps	*the brown fox jumps*	**the brown fox jumps**
TIMES NEW ROMAN (serif)		
the brown fox jumps	*the brown fox jumps*	**the brown fox jumps**
GROTESQUE (sans serif)		
the brown fox jumps	*the brown fox jumps*	**the brown fox jumps**
ROMULUS (serif)		
the brown fox jumps	*the brown fox jumps*	
JULIANA (serif)		
the brown fox jumps	*the brown fox jumps*	

been recorded. Two references in particular, Tinker (1963) and Spencer (1969), provide valuable summaries of these findings. While some studies of this topic, reported by Tinker, have employed threshold measures and have examined the effects of kinds of type when viewed as single letters, the majority of relevant reports are concerned with the influence of type upon the legibility of whole passages and a person's response to them, and therefore have a bearing upon the readability of print.

One typical experiment reported by Tinker sets out to establish which type faces are most easily read in normal conditions. Seven most frequently selected type faces are assessed, using speed of reading as a measure of legibility. There are no significant differences between five of the faces. American Typrewriter and Cloister Black, however, are read more slowly than the others. At a time when more and more schools are using typewritten versions of the children's own work as reading material, the teacher should be fully aware of the influence of type face upon legibility. Selection is becoming increasingly hazardous as the choice of type faces grows. Of particular interest however, is the greater availability of large typewriter faces similar to the type faces used in reading schemes; see the examples overleaf.

In other studies referred to by Tinker, readers' opinions and preferences are taken into account, in addition to speed of reading and eye movement measures. Whilst these opinions show that judged performance are not altogether consistent with the per-

Adler BULLETIN 10 pitch

Dear Sir,

One of the first problems anybody has to face
in business is what to do about typing. This
means two things. The first is buying a
typewriter and the second is hiring a typist

Olympia DISPLAY 10 pitch

DISPLAY is used for tickets, tags, labels and
notices - any work demanding real attention.

A B C D E F G H I   1 2 3 4 5 6 7 8 9

formance on objective measures, Tinker does suggest that there is
a practical value in taking opinions, which editors should not
overlook. This would be an interesting exercise for the teacher to
undertake with children, for not only can the subjective assessment be supported by the measurement of reading speed or
accuracy, but this activity can also be used to increase the child's
insight into his reading skills.

In a further experiment listed by Tinker the correlations between visibility or legibility, perceptibility at a distance, speed of
reading and readers' opinions are examined. The correlations
obtained indicate that visibility and perceptibility measures are
related, but that neither shows any relationship with speed of
reading. The authors further suggest that readers' opinions concerning legibility are based upon visibility and these too correlate
only slightly with speed of reading performance.

Investigations into the legibility of roman lower case and italic
type faces (Paterson and Tinker 1940) have shown that the former

is easier to read and is also more frequently preferred by readers. Luckiesh and Moss (1940) also found that roman lower case and bold face are read more quickly than italic or capitals. The reading of italic print is retarded by marginal changes in conditions more often than roman lower case. In addition, readers consistently express the opinion that roman lower case is easier to read than italic. Tinker suggests that italic print should seldom be used and should be restricted to cases where emphasis is required. There is no apparent difference in the legibility of ordinary lower case and bold face, but roman lower case has been found to be more legible than capitals.

Tinker suggests that it is the contribution which the characteristic cues of letter shapes make towards the overall shape of a word which leads readers to show a preference for various forms of lower case, though there is evidence which suggests that only parts of the letters of a word provide the essential cues for its identification. According to Tinker, any type face which contains cues giving information related to the overall shape of the words, in addition to cues based on line thickness or space within letters, for example, should be preferred.

Studies of this kind, together with investigations into the relative legibility of italic and roman lower case, bold face and mixed type forms, tend to indicate that there are no characteristics of kinds of type which singly will have a serious effect on legibility. Nevertheless, there may be an accumulative effect which has a small but significant effect upon performance. In view of this, the emphasis in future studies may change from the search for a single factor or set of factors which ensure legibility, to a search for optimal conditions and limits outside of which there is a significant deterioration in legibility. The search for optimal conditions is based on the idea that the various individual factors of print interact and that, by combining these factors in particular ways, some arrangements can be found to be more effective than others.

3 INTERACTION OF FACTORS

In view of the modest effects upon legibility attributable to the single variables already referred to, studies of optimal conditions have tended to be concerned with interactions between these and other factors such as leading (which is the amount of space between lines) and line width.

Again, Tinker (1963) has studied the legibility of seven different type sizes. For comparison, examples of the different type sizes are given overleaf in table 2.

Table 2: Examples of different type sizes

6 point
He found the door of his passage open and sprang up the stairs.

8 point
He found the door of his passage open and sprang up the stairs.

9 point
He found the door of his passage open and sprang up the stairs.

10 point
He found the door of his passage open and sprang up the

11 point
He found the door of his passage open and sprang u

12 point
He found the door of his passage open and spr

14 point
He found the door of his passage open and

(NOTE: the part of the type body which is measured in 'points' is indicated in the illustration. 72 points measures approximately 1 inch.)

 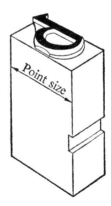

A series of extremely systematic studies led Tinker to conclude that leading has an important effect upon legibility of type, though this was less marked with 12 point. On the basis of these extensive studies of six type sizes set in different line widths and with different leadings, Tinker postulated a series of 'safety zones' within which the three factors might be varied without any significant effect upon legibility. The limits of these 'optimal' conditions are given opposite.

34

Table 3: Safety zones within which type size, line width and leading may be varied without loss of legibility. (The table is not intended to be restrictive since a printer may wish to take into account readers' preferences.)

6 Point Type
    14 pica* line width with 2 to 4 point leading
    21 pica line width with 1 to 4 point leading
    28 pica line width with 2 to 4 point leading

8 Point Type
    14 pica line width with 2 to 4 point leading
    21 pica line width with 2 to 4 point leading
    28 pica line width with 1 to 4 point leading
    36 pica line width with 2 to 4 point leading

9 Point Type
    14 pica line width with 1 to 4 point leading
    18 pica line width with 1 to 4 point leading
    30 pica line width with 1 to 4 point leading

10 Point Type
    14 pica line width with 1 to 4 point leading
    19 pica line width with 2 to 4 point leading
    31 pica line width with 2 point leading (marginal)

11 Point Type
    16 pica line width with 1 to 2 point leading
    25 pica line width with 0 to 4 point leading
    34 pica line width with 1 to 2 point leading

12 Point Type
    17 pica line width with 1 to 4 point leading
    25 pica line width with 0 to 4 point leading
    33 pica line width with 1 to 4 point leading

The significance which should be attached to the use of appropriate type leading and line width is enhanced by Paterson and Tinker's study of the differences in eye movements of subjects reading optimally arranged 10 point type and non-optimally arranged 6 point type. The investigation suggested that non-optimal typographical factors may combine to produce a breakdown of efficient eye movement patterns. The effect of different combinations of point size, line width, and leading may be seen in the three examples below. Only the first example falls within the 'safety zone' for 10 point type mentioned above.

1. *'Pica'* is a printer's measure of line width and is approximately ⅙ of an inch.
2. The table is reprinted, by permission, from *Legibility of Print* by Miles A. Tinker © 1963 Iowa state University Press Ames. Iowa U.S.A.

10 point 14 pica line width 4 point leading

When reading for information, a reader usually intends to extract what he wants from the text, and not merely to absorb what the author presents. For his part, an author, when intent upon transmitting information, must firstly help the reader to perceive the relationship between his own particular information needs and the content and major issues to be dealt with in the book.

10 point 9 pica line width set solid

The initial part of any exposition, therefore, should answer the question, 'What is it all about?' and 'How are these ideas organised so that the various relationships between the different ideas can be readily understood?' In the case of this book, these two questions will be tackled by means of an examination of the concept of readability, and the practical ways in which it has been investigated.

10 point 23 pica line width 6 point leading

The second responsibility of the author is to help the reader by indicating important theoretical and practical applications for the material presented. In the case of this book, it is important to show exactly how an understanding of readability can lead, directly or indirectly, to improvement in the preparation or selection of reading materials so that they are neither too easy nor too difficult for the readership concerned.

The teacher or librarian has little control over the preparation of print though these findings may help in deciding on the suitability of reading material. Professional associations, however, might well think it their business to press publishers to print details of the type faces, size and leading which have been used, together with evidence as to suitability, where particular advantages are claimed. Though again, through professional associations and existing links, such as the National Book League, teachers could play an increased part in the selection of suitable material. There are, however, a number of other factors affecting legibility which can be controlled in the classroom or library.

4 READING CONDITIONS AND LEGIBILITY

Tinker (1963, 1966) has collected evidence concerning the various effects of differences in intensity and direction of illumination upon legibility. The necessity for the elimination of glare and the control of brightness contrast are also considered and a series of prescriptions designed to produce favourable conditions for reading are given. These aspects of legibility are given only a brief mention here.

Wide individual differences in reading conditions, e.g. in the visual acuity of the reader, print size, paper size, the period of time spent reading, etc. make it impossible to lay down final or exact recommendations concerning the intensity of illumination for reading. On the other hand, Tinker reports that control of light distribution, or diffusion, has been found to be of great importance. Loss of efficiency in reading may be caused by unsatisfactory diffusion of light due to glare from highly polished or glazed objects within the field of vision (including the pages of the book). Also, the disturbing effects of bright spots of light above or to the side of the line of vision can impair efficiency. Of course, these factors may interact to produce startling reductions in efficiency in reading, with its consequent increase in misunderstandings and eye-strain, For example, badly diffused illumination is a common phenomenon in reading situations, and when combined with the use of highly glazed paper this has been found seriously to reduce reading speed and hasten fatigue and eye-strain.

A review of research into the effects of brightness contrast has led Tinker to put forward 'brightness ratios' within which conditions for reading are satisfactory. The term 'brightness ratio' usually refers to the relationship between the brightness of two adjacent areas, for example a book and its surrounding table surface. Firstly, the two areas may be equal in brightness. This is a condition which is a theoretical ideal, but which is hardly ever met in practice. In such a case the brightness ratio would be 1 to 1. The second condition occurs when the surrounding area is brighter than the book. In this relatively infrequent situation, visual sensitivity has been found to be markedly reduced. The third and most commonly encountered condition is when the book is brighter than the surrounding area. Tinker, synthesising the evidence, suggests that in this case a ratio of 3 to 1 is very satisfactory, but that beyond 5 to 1 in favour of the book visual sensitivity may be impaired.

Also, Spencer (1969) has illustrated, with some vivid examples, the serious effects on visibility which occur when the angle at which the print is read varies from 90 degrees to the line of vision. The curvature of the page may also lead to considerable distortion. This is particularly common when a book is thick, with a strong spine, but a narrow inner, or gutter, margin. Also, vibration of the print, which will occur when the book is held in the hand, is also shown to have a dramatic effect upon the legibility of the print.

Though often surrounded by unfamiliar technical terms and forms of measurement, generalisations emerge from these studies which may be applied to many everyday reading situations. By taking account of such factors as these when arranging such classroom features as library corners, by constantly attending to the child's reading situation, a teacher can do much to assist the readers, particularly those who are experiencing difficulty in perceiving and decoding letters.

5 MODIFICATIONS IN DESIGN OF TYPE

Tinker's work has helped to draw attention to the important effects of variations in print upon visibility and ease of reading. The results of his experiments have provided a useful framework within which printers might make sensible choices in the preparation of books. All the studies referred to so far deal with modifications of the traditional alphabet. However, many suggestions for more radical redesigning of the alphabet have been put forward. One modern line of investigation is confined to the redesigning of existing characters whereas other approaches seek to increase readability by augmenting the alphabet and increasing the number of printed symbols to correspond to the speech sounds they represent.

The problems of creating alphabets for recognition by machines has led to design and modification of type faces which might well assist human recognition of words, though it appears that little research into these possibilities has been undertaken. Spencer (1969) gives several examples, ranging from alphabets designed in the 1920s to those designed for recognition by computers and those designed for use in television transmissions. The increasing use of print on the screen in the form of subtitles or as an educational aid suggests that this is an area in which studies of legibility and visibility could be particularly profitable.

Of the several examples of typography design in which the alphabet has been augmented, the initial teaching alphabet is perhaps the best known. This is an alphabet which is helpful in learning to read but which permits the reader, when fluent, to transfer on to traditional type faces. In addition to the augmented alphabet, there are many examples of completely new writing systems which are designed on the basis of their relationship to the spoken language and their visibility. Unlike the i.t.a., these alphabets may not bear such a close relationship to the alphabet with which we are familiar, and to which we are tied by tradition. For example, the sentence shown below is printed in a 'fonetic alphabet' designed by Herbert Bayer. This alphabet involves letter forms which are simplified and each letter form or sign refers to a single phoneme. The example is from Bayer 1967.

ʌn ʌlfʌbɛt ko-oʀdinʌetn̦ fonɛtiks ʌnd visin wil̦ bɛ ʌe moʀ ɛfɛktiv tul uf kuṃunikʌetin

Recent developments in techniques of printing and reproduction have created opportunities for the changing of the alphabet and it may be argued that this is no longer a theoretical exercise but a practical necessity. Though practical and economic disadvantages do not apply to all the suggestions which have been put forward, tradition and aesthetics may be the cause of some reluctance to examine and adopt recent developments which would appear to hold out prospects of improved readability of print.

Research into the perceptual processes which determine the way in which we perceive letters in normal text has produced conclusions which should concern typographers and teachers. It is now well established, for example, that a fluent reader processes only part of what he sees. The more fluent he is, the less he actually needs to see of each letter, in order to identify correctly.

Several researchers describe visual decoding factors which relate to later fluency.

Huey (1968) first drew attention to the fact that the upper coastline of a line of print is more informative than the lower coastline to a fluent reader.

Gold space stops cloudy rooms

Sluggish bread likes thin frills

Dry feelings chew cloudy ideas

Gold space stops cloudy rooms

Sluggish bread likes thin frills

Dry feelings chew cloudy ideas

More recently Kolers (1968 and 1969) has demonstrated that for a person reading systematically from left to right the right hand side of the letters is more informative.

Gold space stops cloudy rooms

Sluggish bread likes thin frills

Dry feelings chew cloudy ideas

Bold space acts clourly ...

Sluggisn read lices tnin Frills

Dr Feelings nev cloud/ideas

On the basis of his experimental findings, Kolers proposes an alphabet which might improve legibility for the reader, since it permits the reader to exploit basic decoding skills. In particular, Kolers argues that type faces which emphasise bold down-strokes for the Roman alphabet impede smooth visual processing since the skilled reader utilises the right hand side of a letter more than the left. In his alphabet, distinguishing clues to recognition are arranged on the right of the letter to assist fluency while at the same time acknowledging the aesthetic aspects of print design. In the design of any new type face, therefore, the production of more clearly visible and legible print may be made possible by the incorporation of the above findings when designing the shape of the characters. Similarly, augmented alphabets, such as i.t.a., could be profitably modified to increase the ease with which the letters may be recognised and responded to.

We have seen that a number of factors in the print and in the reading conditions interact to produce marked effects upon the readability of books. While some of these influences are within the direct control of the teacher, other important factors are not, and it is argued that the print available to the teacher could be improved if the relevant research findings were incorporated into the preparation of reading materials. The print is a set of symbols which stand for a spoken language, however, and it is in the relationship between spoken language and print that other factors affecting readability will be found.

Chapter 4   Sounds and Letters

We learn to respond to language at a variety of levels—from complete statements down to single speech sounds: for example, in listening to a lecture or talk, we react to the overall plan. This is the scheme or structure which is often, but not always, described by the speaker and within which we expect different topics to be discussed. Within this plan, we also follow the particular argument and within the arguments we respond to particular ideas. In addition, we react to shorter speech patterns such as single sentences, phrases, and also single words. Then, at the most primitive level, we react to the raw material of which language is composed—sounds. We are thus responding simultaneously at a number of different levels of cognitive organisation. We can easily see that the same set of influences will also be involved when we speak, and when we read.

The objective here is not to catalogue exhaustively the various analyses of patterns of speech, but to describe briefly the first of four units into which language is usually divided for analysis and which affect our performance in reading, and thus readability. The other three units are discussed in Chapters 5, 6 and 7.

1 SOUNDS

The number of speech sounds used in the English language is approximately forty-five. Those speech sounds which we use to distinguish words are called phonemes. Unfortunately, while the phonemes are limited in number, there are many variations within individual phonemes which occur in normal speech. These differences in speech, which do not serve to distinguish between phonemes, are called allophonic variations. The range of sounds which we categorise as examples of the same phoneme may be very wide.

Thus, for example, the phoneme /p/ as pronounced in 'pin' and 'spin' is very different in sound. Although the /p/ in 'pin' is heavily aspirated while in 'spin' it is not, the difference in sound is not regarded by the listener as informative. On the other hand, the difference between the sounds of the phoneme /w/ in 'witch' and 'which' may convey a difference in meaning. Generally speaking, this contrast is not made in English though it does occur in Scottish dialects. On the other hand, there are many examples of sounds in which the listener can only judge the meaning of the word from contextual clues as the words sound similar. Common examples of these homophones are 'through' and 'threw' and 'two' and 'too'. In other cases listeners have difficulty because one word may have several meanings attached to it, i.e. there is no distinction to be found either in the way it is pronounced or in the spelling. In the case of these homonyms the listener must again refer to context to establish the meaning of the word. The ambiguities caused by homonyms and homophones lead not only to confusion in understanding speech but also to difficulties in reading.

The list of phonemes of the English language includes all those elements which go to make up words, i.e. those parts of the language commonly referred to as consonants, diphthongs and vowels. These phonemes are pieces from which larger units are built in a specific temporal sequence. They are referred to as segmental, since they are the units into which a continuous flow of speech is analysed and broken up, just as letters are segmental, and are the units used to represent in print the continuous flow of speech.

We also use other aspects of sound production to convey meaning. Stress and pitch both play a part in our understanding of words. When we speak, stress and pitch occur at the same time as segmental phonemes and so are called simultaneous or suprasegmental phonemes. Stress refers to the relative intensity with which a syllable is pronounced. For example, consider the word 'entrance'. If the first syllable is stressed the sounds refer to an opening or point of entry. If the second syllable is stressed, however, the sounds mean to throw into a trance or overwhelm. Thus suprasegmental phonemes are also critical in word identification in some cases. Such instances are, however, relatively infrequent, and as our writing system does not signal them, the reader must be capable of using context clues and his personal experience of using stress to convey meaning.

Pitch refers to the relative height of the tone with which a syllable is spoken. In Chinese, for example, differences in relative pitch distinguish between the meanings of words. In our language the influence of pitch is not so marked, but a rising tone of voice over long speech patterns is used to indicate a feeling of doubt or disbelief. Similarly, we use a rising pitch in the repetition of words to convey differences in sense: for example, when we say 'No! No! NO!' we convey a difference in meaning by altering the pitch. When spoken, the third repetition usually leaves the listener in no doubt as to what was meant. (Notice how, in print, differences in pitch have to be inferred from context, unusual print patterns and punctuation.)

In addition to the sounds we make, there are pauses or junctures. These may also alter the meaning of a word or the sense of an utterance. As an example of this the reader should say aloud 'a location' and 'allocation'. It will be seen how difficult it is to distinguish the alternatives in normal speech, though the meaning can be indicated by artificially emphasising the juncture. Here, at least, print is more helpful than speech as word boundaries are signalled by spacing.

2 SEQUENCES OF SOUNDS

Of course, phonemes are not to be regarded mainly as separate sounds. In speech they are run together to form sequences. Much of the meaning which the flow of speech has for us is based upon the information which we glean from the sequence of sounds. As we have seen, the range of phonemes which we use in English is restricted. The ways in which clusters occur are also restricted. Thus, there are certain sound combinations which, although pronounceable, never, or rarely, occur in English, e.g. eegn, oonk, etc. Conversely, there are certain conditions which occur frequently, e.g. ing, pre, ent, etc. The combinations of phonemes which we use and their position in different words are characteristics of language which a fluent speaker must be able to predict and react to habitually if he is to be able to cope efficiently with reading situations.

It is true of all languages that there are groups of phonemes which occur more frequently than others. Certain of these combinations, or clusters of phonemes occur in several languages but each language contains clusters which are very unfamiliar in others. Indeed, we can often make very accurate predictions about the nationality of a stranger by noting the unusual sound patterns in their speech. In this way, when we describe German as a 'guttural' language we are noting patterns of consonants and vowels which are different from those which occur in English. Similarly, our frequent description of Italian as 'musical' or 'lilting' is based upon our reaction to differences in the use of pitch and to the use in Italian of a more restricted pattern of consonant clusters than in English.

The frequency with which clusters of phonemes occur influences our response not only to foreign languages but to differences in our own. In our language, for example, consonant-vowel-consonant clusters occur more frequently than clusters involving three consonants, and the cluster of sounds 'df' is less common than 'st'. As fluent speakers, we have learned to use these factors to assist us in recognising old words and attacking new ones. 'Supercallifragalisticexpialodocious' is less daunting to an English speaker than a phrase such as 'this sixth sixtieth', because of the differences in the frequency of occurrence of the sequences of phonemes.

We can see that the frequently occuring clusters of phonemes are also usually easier to pronounce. It is easy to appreciate the breakdown of communication which would occur if the most frequent phoneme clusters were also the most difficult to pronounce! Pronunciability has been shown to affect the speed of recognition of words and the rate of learning new words (Gibson *et al.* 1963). This in turn has an effect upon the readability of a passage, in that fluency and ease of reading are used as measures of readability.

A further characteristic of many clusters of phonemes is that they generally occur in certain positions. For example, the sounds represented by 'tion' and 'ing' usually occur at the end of a word while the consonant cluster 'str' is encountered at the beginning or middle but never the end of a word. Knowledge of this kind of phonemic rule is useful in determining, in the flow of speech, where a word ends and a new one begins, and in establishing the grammatical class and function of the words. Such 'knowledge' is, of course, that kind of knowledge which affects the ease with which we read a passage and which need not even be consciously acquired or processed.

The aspects of the sound system or phonology of our language described above do not reflect the full extent and complexity of this type of analysis. They are intended to exemplify some of the features of those characteristics of language which teachers of reading recognise as influential in learning to read. Failure to respond to these basic properties of language when they are encountered in print may be a contributory cause of reading difficulty and thus a factor influencing readability. This point will be taken up again in the chapter on assessment of readability.

3 READING LETTERS

When we turn to the relationship between printed symbols and the sounds which they represent, several points emerge which can be seen to affect the extent to which a person finds material readable. It was noted in the discussion of language that we use a limited number of only forty-five phonemes to convey meaning. We might expect that a similar number of written symbols would be used to correspond to these sounds. With only twenty-six letters in the alphabet, it is clear that some of the sounds of English must be represented by combinations of letters. These combinations of letters and single letters which represent particular speech sounds are called graphemes.

When we read letters, we are matching a series of visual cues to a series of sounds. This involves the application of two complimentary processes which must have been learned previously through listening and speaking. On the one hand, the individual must have learned to pick out one sound from the flow of speech, while on the other hand, he must also have learned to blend sounds together. This analysis and synthesis of speech sounds has seen shown by Gibson *et al.* (1963) to play an important part in reading. It affects both learning to read and the development of fluency.

The ability to pronounce a letter correctly depends on our recognition of the important clues in the letters. As has been mentioned earlier, when the letters are in a sequence we must use a left to right eye movement to decode them and within this movement we must also respond to letter shape and orientation. Consider the following groups of letter: o, c, e, and b, h, k. Each letter is different from its neighbour in shape. This difference is used to indicate which sound the letter is equivalent to. With normal vision there is usually no difficulty in making correct identifications. On the other hand, the groups of letters   G, g, g, and   T, t, t, t,   show differences which might be taken, by a learner, to indicate a difference in sound. In this case, however, the reader must learn that the differences in letter shape are not indicative of differences in sound. Clearly, the learning of sound to letter equivalence is not altogether straightforward. The existence of these anomalies increases the 'learning load' for the beginning reader. It must also, presumably, affect the readability at a later stage, particularly in the case of the inadequate reader.

The task of learning the equivalence of sound and letters is rendered more difficult by the confusions in letter recognition which will arise. As well as letter shapes, we also use letter orientation as a clue to identification. In the letters b, p, d, q, or n and u, for example, the different letters in each set share a common shape and differ only in their orientation on the page. Even if serifs are used, the principal means of identifying these letters is orientation. Vernon (1957) and Merritt (1969a) account for common reversals which are made in reading these letters by pointing out that the use of orientation to distinguish between letters is in direct conflict with the child's earlier experience in which the child learned that an object keeps its unique identity in spite of being presented in many different positions and orientations. They argue, in other words, that a child develops a 'set' to respond to shape, and to ignore orientation, in defining objects. The occurrence of so-called reversals in learning, therefore, must be attributed to an unfortunate aspect of the design of our alphabet rather than some kind of maturational factor in the development of children.

Kolers and Perkins (1969a) have shown that these cues to letter recognition interact to facilitate identification. In an experiment using specially constructed texts they showed that speed of letter naming may be accounted for by an interaction between the direction of scan and the orientation of the letters. They also report (Kolers and Perkins 1969b) that errors in letter naming may be accounted for by the same interaction. The further investigation and research of this aspect of letter recognition should be useful to the teacher in suggesting teaching techniques which would assist the child in its learning. It will be a pity, perhaps, if such studies do not lead to modifications in alphabet design.

4 READING GROUPS AND SEQUENCES OF LETTERS

The reader of English faces a task which is not present where the different graphemes used in the writing of the language correspond as they do in some languages, for example Italian, with reasonable consistency, to particular phonemes. Our spelling system being what it is, there are literally thousands of graphemes which are used to represent the forty-five phonemes mentioned earlier. The reader must learn that many phonemes are represented by single letters but, in addition, he must learn that many clusters of letters when grouped together represent only one phoneme. Apart from the confusion that this causes, the reader has to cope with a considerably greater 'learning load' in learning to read in English than he would have to cope with in learning to read many other languages.

Fortunately, many of the graphemes which use more than one letter are used to represent particular sounds consistently: for example, 'tion', 'shr', and 'ck' correspond consistently to particular sounds. A fluent reader obviously utilises these consistencies to assist in reading quickly and in attacking new words. If we can utilise these consistencies then even nonsense words such as 'cubdention' or 'dinshring' can be attacked and read even though the reader may be unable to attach meaning to the word.

On the other hand, those phoneme-grapheme correspondences which are not so consistent may give rise to confusion and reading difficulty. For example, in the words 'only', 'on', 'done', 'to', 'whom', and 'women', the letter 'o' represents a different sound on each occasion. We can see that knowledge of the various alternatives does not help the reader to deal with new words. Consider, for example, the different ways in which a nonsense word such as 'wother' can be pronounced, when the letter 'o' can take on so many values. Also, the reader might like to write out the alternative spellings for the pronunciation of 'foeshent'— in this way, it will soon be appreciated that many variations are available. In the absence of a dictionary or a teacher, how is the reader to know which is the correct one?

When reading, we are frequently exposed to another type of confusion. If we consider the words 'I', 'high', 'height' and 'my', the phoneme /ai/ has been represented by different graphemes. Here, the problem to the reader is that each inconsistent spelling must be learned by repetition, though he may increase his accuracy by using other wider contextual or semantic clues.

From experimental results we can see the part played by phoneme-grapheme correspondences in reading. Using nonsense words and pseudowords, Gibson *et al.* (1962) prepared lists in which the degree of phoneme-grapheme correspondence varied. They found that when the lists were exposed at different speeds, subjects recognised most quickly the words which had the highest spelling to sound relationship. Also the words identified most quickly were most easily pronounced. These results emphasise the importance in reading of learning about groups of letters and also the close relationship between reading and speech. Fluent reading will depend upon the degree to which the print is made up of close phoneme-grapheme correspondences, and the extent to which the reader can use his knowledge of correspondences to deal with the new words which he meets. A reader who is unable to respond to these correspondences may still be able to read the print but must depend for his success upon other clues.

Of course, the spelling or pronunciation rules themselves are not so straightforward as they appear. In addition to rules concerning the spelling of single sounds we must learn that the position of a group of letters in a word may affect its pronunciation, as in the case of 'ghost' and 'enough'.

The literature on learning to read contains many similar examples. These inconsistencies of phoneme-grapheme correspondence which will affect the readability of print are used by the protagonists of spelling reform and of particular methods of teaching reading to provide support for their arguments. While such factors may not be of great importance to the fluent reader, inconsistencies of this kind must affect readability to a significant extent in the case of a young child or a child who is not making satisfactory progress in reading.

Just as we are used to hearing phonemes in different clusters and sequences, so we learn to recognise clusters of letters which make up graphemes and also to respond to the sequences of graphemes. The way in which letter sequences are formed may have a marked effect upon how well we can read, as the examples below should indicate. Read each series and decide which letter seems to round it off most appropriately.

i a g s r h t a c ( )
ii d d d d d d d d ( )
iii c d e f g h i j ( )
iv s e l e c t i o ( )
v p r u g i l e n ( )

i The first series may cause the reader some confusion and difficulty since any letter would appear to fit. In fact, any letter can be regarded as correct since the sequence is a random series. Neither the individual letters nor the sequence of letters offer a basis on which to make a sensible prediction. The guesses of some children learning to read suggest that they think that sounds in print follow a similar haphazard sequence. Of particular interest in this example is the uncertainty, confusion and frustration which we experience when we cannot find a basis on which to predict the next letter. If we were to continue to find the letters impossible to predict, we should soon declare the print unintelligible and stop reading. Teachers of reading will have encountered many individuals who were deterred from persisting because of their inability to find sense in the letter sequences.

ii This is an unusual series. The consistency of the letters leads one to predict a 'd'. As we proceed along the line and find each letter the same, each successive sound becomes less informative since it adds nothing to what has gone before; it merely confirms the series. We reach the point in such a series where our expectancy is such that we would be extremely surprised if the next letter was not a 'd'! Our response to this highly predictable series lacks the uncertainty and frustration of series *i* above.

iii We solve this series by referring to our alphabet. Our familiarity with this arrangement of sounds makes the letter 'k' highly predictable. Our knowledge of the invariant nature of the alphabet assists us in making a very confident guess about the next sound in the series. We find our alphabet a useful series. It makes cataloguing as simple as A, B, C, but it is not a sequence found frequently in language or in running text.

iv The choice of the letter 'n' is highly predictable. In this case, our prediction is based upon our knowledge of phonemic sequences, the spellings which usually represent them and the meaning of the word. We hear the ending 'ion' very frequently in everyday speech and in reading the letters i-o-n have come to be associated with the sounds. The use of these linguistic and spelling rules makes this particular prediction easy and frequent. As in the case of series *ii*, the letter is so predictable that we would tend to disbelieve any alternative offered and assume that it was a printer's error.

v In this case, there will be a tendency to complete the series with 't' or perhaps 'd' or 's'. Although this is a new word, albeit a nonsense word, we can make confident predictions about the final letter using the knowledge of sequences of sounds and spelling patterns which was used to complete series *iv* and which was referred to earlier.

The ease with which we complete the last two examples is an indication of the frequency with which those graphemes occur in print but also the extent to which the reader is familiar with them and can manipulate them. In order to complete the series, we scan the letters for information which will help us to read. Obviously, if the letters follow a familiar pattern we do not need to look at them all since we can predict what some of them will be. If letters are unnecessary for this reason, they are said to be redundant.

It is possible to assess the redundancy of letters in a series in a mathematical way by measuring the number of times one letter follows the others: for example, a measure of the redundancy of the letter 'c' would be obtained by taking a sample of text and calculating the frequency with which 'c' follows each letter of the alphabet, or a punctuation mark or a space between words. The more frequently it follows a particular letter, punctuation mark or space the more redundant the letter 'c' is when following that letter. From the point of view of the readability of the text the examination of letter redundancy could be profitably undertaken by children. In an activity similar to 'code-breaking', the predictive value of letter sequences can be readily displayed and incorporated into the child's reading skills.

We may say that the more unfamiliar the reader is with the individual words the less fluent his reading will be. This will be due in part to the difficulty the reader will have in word attack when faced with letter sequences of relatively low frequency.

Chapter 5 Spoken Words and Printed Words

The flow of speech is divided not only into the units of sound which we have considered but also into other larger units which convey meaning to the listener. These larger units—words—may be described either in terms of the part they play within the rules of grammar, i.e. their syntactic function, or they may be examined in terms of the meaning which they convey, i.e. their semantic function. These two distinct aspects of words in a language are equally important and are in addition interdependent. Consider 'This is a grave affair' and 'One foot in the grave'. In these examples the word 'grave' can be seen to have two different grammatical functions as well as two distinct meanings. The units of speech described below will therefore have to be looked at from the point of view of both their syntactic and semantic functions. This distinction is reflected in the organisation of this section.

In the preceding section, it was possible to maintain a close parallel between the examination of sounds and letters and their bearing upon readability. However, such a close link is difficult to maintain since words have more functions than letters, that is to say, we respond to a word at a number of levels. Consequently, in order to appreciate the way in which the content, structure and sequencing of spoken words affect readability, it is necessary to describe certain aspects of language in some detail. Though the ideas described may not be closely related to the subject of readability at each stage, it is hoped that this discussion will be valuable when factors involved in reading words are considered.

Firstly, then, the grammatical function of words will be examined and then the way in which meaning is attached to words. This will be followed by an examination of how these, and other attributes of words combine to affect readability.

1 THE FUNCTION OF WORDS

Words such as 'grammar' and 'syntax' may deter some readers since they may remind them of many hours spent at school learning interminable and often incomprehensible rules which seemed to have little relevance to one's speech when they had been learned. Happily, the traditional approach to the grammatical analysis of language has been modified by the results of recent research into linguistics and those aspects of syntax which are relevant to teachers are more interesting and more readily understood.

We are all familiar with the categorising of language by 'parts of speech', i.e. nouns, verbs, adverbs and so on. Another system for categorising words relevant to this context involves sorting words into only two categories: words which convey meaning, called 'content' words, and words which have a grammatical function. Nouns, verbs and adjectives would be examples of 'content' words, while conjunctions and prepositions would be classified as 'function' words. Both these systems can be used to classify any word but of interest here is the psychological significance of the classification.

An experiment by Glanzer (1962) demonstrated how our learning and remembering of words is affected by our syntactic categories. Glanzer gave his subjects the task of learning pairs of words—nonsense words had to be paired with either content or function words. His subjects found it easier to learn to associate nonsense words with content words than with function words. For instance YIG—FOOD and MEF—THINK were more readily associated than TAH—OF and KEX—AND. In an extension of this paired associate test, subjects were asked to learn triplets of words in which the content and function words were sandwiched between nonsense syllables. Here, the subjects found it easier to learn sequences such as TAH—OF—ZUM and KEX—AND—WOJ faster than YIG—FOOD—SEB and MEF—THINK—JAT. In this series of tests, the subjects were able to use the function words to bond the triplets together as if it were a natural unit in everyday speech. The ability to use certain words to bind sentences together and so influence fluency will clearly affect the rate and accuracy with which a person reads and, as a result, will influence the readability of print. Similarly, variations in the proportions of content and function words and the way in which they are arranged will affect the readability of different texts.

Unless the reader is a specialist in English, he would expect the word to remain the next unit in size above the phoneme to be used as a basis for analysis. In fact, however, other smaller units called morphemes, have been suggested by linguists as the second most basic unit for investigating all languages. These morphemes are the smallest units of speech which convey meaning to a listener. 'Good', 'un', 'hot', 'ing' are all examples of morphemes. As the examples show, a morpheme may be made up of a number of phonemes.

In some situations, a single sound may be a morpheme whereas the same phoneme in other situations does not have this function. For example, in the word 'zone' the 'z' is merely a phoneme contrasting zone from other similar sounds such as loan, and cone. It has no grammatical function. However, in the word 'boys' although the 'z' sounded at the end of the word is a phoneme, it is also a morpheme. It distinguishes boy (singular) from boys (plural) and so it has a meaning, i.e. 'more than one'. It is also to be found on a number of other words fulfilling the same grammatical function.

The importance of morphemes in reading can be easily appreciated. In the example given above, the morpheme 'z' in 'boys' is important, not only because of the grammatical information it conveys but also because of the sense or meaning which it conveys. Morphemes may be seen to signal both function and content of a word. A reader must make a response to both aspects of this element of words if he is to develop his fluency.

Additionally, particular morphemes often occur in a fixed position in a word and convey the same information whatever word they are attached to. Learning to respond to the consistency of these elements of language is a significant step in the development of fluency and comprehension. Teachers often help children to overcome this source of difficulty by signalling certain morphemes using additional cues, such as diacritical marks, and by arranging exercises which involve the discrimination of consistent morphemes such as the plural 's' given above. The range, frequency of occurrence and consistency of morphemes could influence the readability of different texts.

The use of the morpheme as a unit of analysis has revealed a number of linguistic patterns which are as strictly regular in their forms and sequences as words and which are helpful in analysing language. For the purpose of this text, however, the next unit of analysis to be considered remains the word, as many morphemes are also words and therefore reflect the linguistic patterns revealed in morphemic analysis. Additionally, in reading and writing the use of spaces to separate words rather than morphemes is more understandable to the reader.

2 THE MEANINGS OF WORDS

The meanings which individuals attach to single words has been most extensively studied by means of word association tests: a list of stimulus words is given to a person and the number of words or the type of words given in response is used as a measure of the significance or meaning of those stimulus words. Several studies have shown that types of word associations change with increasing age. Children will tend to give such responses as 'dark—night', 'soft—pillow' and 'mountain—high', while adult responses will tend to be of the type 'table—chair', 'dark—light', or 'mountain—hill'. The responses of the children have a linguistic basis, i.e. the continuity of words and the frequency with which they occur together; whereas adult responses have a semantic basis, i.e. the contrast or similarity of word meanings and their homogeneity in terms of parts of speech. Brown and Berko (1960) conclude from this and other results that the development of word associations from those based upon the frequency of co-occurrence is necessary if meaning is to develop.

It is clear however that the study of the meaning of single words is restrictive as much meaning is conveyed by contextual cues given by the adjacent words in a phrase or sentence. It is also necessary to examine what is meant by the 'meaning' of meaning, in view of the variations and confusions which exist.

Consider the following examples:

i She means a lot to me.

ii That sneezing means that you have flu.

iii Democracy means government of the people, by the people, for the people.

iv Do you understand the meaning of Bach's music?

In the first case, 'means' is used in the sense of 'to be of importance' or 'of value'. Though in frequent usage this is a sense or meaning with which we are not particularly concerned here. In the second example, the word is used to convey 'is a sign of' or 'a signal that'. In the third example, we are using the word 'means' in a more familiar way. It is being used as a symbol to stand for a thing or a concept which has particular characteristics. In the last example, 'means' is used to refer to an emotional reaction or aesthetic appeal which music might have.

We can readily appreciate the confusion which arises out of these differences in definition when we come to describe meaning in language. To assist in clarifying this problem, and to increase our understanding of the meaning of language, psychologists and linguists usually draw a distinction between words used as 'signs' (example *ii*) and words used as 'symbols' (examples *iii* and *iv*).

a **Signs and symbols**

Signs, in general, are events which direct attention to or are indicative of other events and things. When these events are related naturally or casually, they are referred to as signs. They elicit an anticipation of a subsequent event. For example, we take a fall in air pressure as indicative of worsening weather; or thunder may be taken as a sign that the gods are angry. When we use words to communicate to animals we are using them as signs. To Pavlov's famous dogs a bell was a sign for dinner, and when they heard it they showed a signal reaction and salivated. Similarly, to a pet dog, the words 'home' or 'walk' act as signs and evince a similar signal reaction. We can see in children a similar response to words as signs. Indeed, the process by which dogs and other animals learn to respond to stimuli has been used, particularly by Skinner, to explain how words acquire meaning. Carroll (1964) gives a brief but clear description of the stages involved in this learning process.

On the other hand, a symbol elicits a response which is the same as the response elicited by the object, person or event which it represents. For example, respect for an altar or relic may come to represent a respect for God. Similarly, when events are related or grouped according to some convention the means by which they are represented are called symbols. Examples of these conventional symbols are the agreed representations for churches, roads, etc. on maps. However, whereas map symbols often do bear some stylised resemblance to the things they represent, the sounds used to represent things or experiences are almost wholly based upon arbitrary convention. In only a small proportion of cases do the sounds in a word bear a close relationship to the object they represent, for example, 'cuckoo'. Meanings would be very much easier to learn if more words were like this. Symbols, then, may be regarded as a special kind of sign and if we accept the distinction drawn above, the vast majority of words are symbols. The teacher will recognise the effect which this distinction has upon teaching the meanings of words. 'Signs' are much more easily taught than 'symbols' and the teaching of the symbolic use of words often involves reference to analogies which are not always easy for a child to understand.

When we are talking to children and helping them to learn our language, we often try to assist them by introducing them to objects and inventing words in which the sounds used are related to the object in some way, for example, 'wuff wuff', 'ding dong' or 'cockadoodloo'. In these cases, the sound system itself is being used to convey meaning. Apart from these artificially produced examples, some conventional words are onomatopoeic in this way. Such words as 'cuckoo' referred to above or 'splutter' show some degree of relationship between the arrangement of sounds and the object or event to which they refer. Unfortunately, very few words exhibit this relationship and therefore the sound system itself is of very little use in establishing the meanings of words.

Although single words are only affected in a small way, ono-
matopoeia will be seen to affect the meaning of language in other
ways, but loses much of its effect in print unless the appropriate
stress and pitch can be identified and responded to.

The most usual situation in which we say a word has a meaning
is when we use it to stand for an object, person or event in the
outside world, or for a concept or state of feeling in the internal
world of our thoughts and emotions. The thing which a word
symbol stands for is usually called its referent. The referent of the
symbol 'Rembrandt' is the one person renowned for a particular
set of portrait paintings and the referent of 'chair' is whatever
individual chair or chairs the word brings to mind in a particular
context. Of course, no two people have exactly the same experience or mental picture of either 'Rembrandt' or 'chair' but each
uses the same word symbol for it. In this way a given symbol comes
to be attached by large numbers of people to a particular thing or
class of things. We then regard the word as being part of the
language of the community.

One result of this linking of a particular symbol with the object
it symbolises, or referent, as it is called, is that it often becomes
very strongly identified with it. This phenomenon of identifying
the word with the object sometimes leads to a belief in adults, as
well as in children, that a thing carries only one true name and
any alternative is wrong and even 'immoral'. Carried to its
extreme, in some primitive communities there is even the idea
that knowing the name of an enemy or a spirit will carry with it
some sort of power or control. In civilised communities also, we
tend to have a high regard for someone who can give a name to
something. To be able to give names to whole classes of things
such as 'genetics', 'schizophrenics' or 'dyslexics' is often taken
unquestioningly by a listener as evidence of a knowledge of the
true essence of the thing that has been named. It is worth examining the relationship between knowing the word and knowing its
meaning a little further.

Imagine that, as an uninformed city dweller, you are on a tour
of the country and ask of a nearby guide, 'What kind of thing is
that?' and the guide replies, 'It's an anticline'. This reply implies
that you have learned something essential about the thing—that
you have learned what kind of thing it is. Suppose you decide on
your return home to find out more about the 'anticline'. In a
dictionary you find a definiton such as 'a geological feature; a
ridge on which the strata lean against each other, and from which
they slope down in opposite directions'. If you continue to define
the unknown words and refer to geological texts you eventually
arrive at a visual representation (photograph or drawing) or a

thorough verbal description of the thing you asked about in the first place!

What the guide really told you had nothing to do with the essence of anticlines—it was the name which English speaking people give to the kind of thing you were pointing to. This may be a useful piece of information, but it does not add anything to the meaning which the anticline has for you. The point of this example is that the reader who learns the names and even strings of related names, may be mesmerised into thinking he knows what he is talking about when he uses the words. This kind of reaction, however, can not be considered to be comprehension of the words.

It is unfortunate that this should tend to occur, since much time in the classroom is spent undoing the misunderstandings which are caused when children attach words to the wrong referents and when they are unable to relate words directly to experiences which permit the meaning of the word to be learned, Propagandists of different kinds exploit this tendency by means of the careful choice of words or references to 'expert' opinion, which the victim of the propaganda has no way of checking. Clearly if we are to assess readability we must be concerned with something more than the more facile responses that a text may elicit.

b Denotation and connotation

If we observe a number of examples of an object, such as a chair, we can establish a series of critical characteristics present in all the examples we are looking at and which enable us to distinguish between chairs and other objects. Although other objects may have some characteristics of chairs they are not included in the definition because some critical element is missing. The denotative meaning of a word is the sum of all the attributes which must be present if the word is to be used in the language of the community.

In many cases the denotative meaning of a word can be established by observation or by pointing. The denotative meaning of 'chair' can be derived by looking at various referents and having critical aspects pointed out. Proper names, such as Winston Churchill, have denotative meaning since they indicate certain referents with identifiable characteristics. The denotative meaning of other words, however, cannot be established by pointing to referents in the outside world. Nevertheless, words like 'dragon' or 'goblin' or 'centaur' are used meaningfully even though the people using the words know that such things do not exist. They can be meaningful because all their separate parts can be described by means of terms which do have referents in the real world, e.g. legs, arms, nostrils, fins, etc. and these referents can be illustrated by means of imaginative drawings. The referents of words like 'truth' and 'justice' or 'good' and 'beautiful' on the other hand refer to mental constructs or inner emotional states, and so cannot be observed or pointed out by others—a fact which has led to many disputes over meaning. These disputes are clarified, but not resolved, by pointing to examples of actions or objects which tend to elicit the psychological states to which the terms refer.

Connotation has two aspects. On the one hand, it refers to the qualities which a person uses in giving a name to a class or category of referents, and on the other hand it refers to the emotional or affective responses which a word produces. Suppose we have seen a number of examples of similar living things, and after defining their qualities, given them a name: birds. As we meet more and more examples of birds, we notice that in addition to the qualities which we used to define this class of living thing, they have one or more accompanying qualities, e.g. coloured plumage, ability to fly. It does not matter how many birds we see with these accompanying qualities for it does not affect their membership of the class. For example, the vast majority of birds can fly but this is still not a defining attribute since ostriches and emus do not fly.

The failure to distinguish between defining and accompanying qualities causes great confusion and anomalies when we come to use the words in speech. We can talk of white blackbirds or 'comics' which are full of horror, violence and death. These possible anomalies are the result of changes in connotation which take place slowly over long periods of time. The reader will probably be able to think of other anomalies which produce similar misconceptions and distort the meanings of words to a considerable extent.

When we are asked what a word means, we usually attempt to describe the characteristics of the referent. If the word is 'dog' then we say what a dog looks like, and a series of definitions would show great similarities. On the other hand, if we are asked what significance the word 'dog' has for us, then there would be wide differences in our answers which would reflect our previous pleasant or unpleasant experiences of dogs or the strength of our desire to own a dog. The connotative meanings which we attach to language play a critical part in conversation and also in reading.

In addition to denotation and connotation, very often words may carry additional meanings which refer to ways of thinking and reasoning. For example, we have seen that a number of short

English words, such as 'and', 'but' and 'or' have a very important grammatical function, they may also be seen to have a semantic function.

Consider the use of these three words in the following sentences:

i Jim and Fred were there.
ii All were saved but one.
iii Pen or pencil will do.

In the first example, 'and' serves not only as a conjunction, it corresponds to the logical concept of inclusion. In the second sentence, 'but' corresponds to the concept of exclusion, while 'or' in the third sentence signifies equivalence. The extent to which we can place meanings like this upon this kind of word will determine the meaning which we can obtain from sentences whether spoken or written. This kind of meaning is very difficult to grasp for children lacking experience in logical thinking and yet, in some contexts, the logical concept may be necessary for comprehension. The readability of a text, then, will be appreciably affected by the complexity of the relationships introduced by logical meanings of this kind.

3 READING WORDS

Words, considered separately or in sequences, are the elements of print which have been most frequently studied in the assessment of readability. We have seen that the word is not the only useful unit into which speech may be divided. Indeed, in the flow of speech, it is often unnecessary to separate the language into separate words, because contextual cues and redundant passages enable us to understand what is said without having to divide the flow of sounds into smaller units. In print, however, the words are already separated by spaces or punctuation marks whether this is helpful or not. What then are the characteristics of words in print which might affect the readability of a book? Also, how are these characteristics dealt with by the reader to produce successful reading?

One consequence of using language as we do is that some words occur in speech more frequently than others. Similarly, of course, some words occur in print more frequently than others. Several lists have been compiled showing the frequency of words appearing in different kinds of print and in the spoken language of adults and children. Perhaps the most famous is Thorndike's Teacher's Word Book, last revised in 1944. The systematic tabulation of the frequency with which words occur has been of practical usefulness. In particular, it has permitted us to examine the relationship between frequency of words in speech and in texts, and the effect of this relationship upon readability.

The frequency with which words occur in print will, as we saw earlier, influence the performance of the reader. Since the opportunities for encountering frequent words are increased, there is a better chance of them being learned. However, many of the most frequent words are boring function words and, also, function words may be more often guessed than recognised. In spite of these drawbacks, word frequencies are often manipulated to facilitate learning to read. For example, a recent study of word frequencies conducted by McNally and Murray (1962) has provided the basis for a popular reading scheme.

A further point in considering the effects of differences in word frequency is also related to the classification of words as either 'function' or 'content'. The 'function' words referred to earlier tend to have had Anglo-Saxon origins and therefore tend to be short. 'Content' words which convey meaning however are much more often derived from Latin and Greek, and consequently tend to be polysyllabic. In addition, the meaning of the short function words are acquired through frequent exposure and habitual practice, whereas the meanings of the less familiar and longer words have to be more systematically learned. This may often be a difficult problem since these longer words tend to be less frequent in everyday speech than in print.

Zipf (1935) produced a mathematical expression which reflected this relationship between word frequency and length. This was described as his 'law of abbreviation' and is exemplified by the tendency for words to be shortened with increasing use. For example, 'omnibus' has been abbreviated to 'bus' and 'television' to 'tele' or TV. Also specialists speaking to one another often abbreviate words and even phrases into letter sequences. These sequences are usually carefully prepared, are easy to pronounce, and thus assist communication and memory. PAL and SECAM may be very meaningful and easily identifiable to television engineers while students of economics might be happier with GATT, EFTA and COMECON. However, an essential distinction must be drawn between word frequency and familiarity. Although frequency is obviously a factor which will determine familiarity, the individual preferences and experiences of the reader will restrict its effect. Due to specialised reading, some words, which are extremely infrequent in general word lists, will be familiar to some individuals while some words occurring frequently may be unfamiliar. The fact that a word comes high on a word frequency list is no consolation to a child attempting to read it when he first encounters it. The absence of a close relationship between familiarity and frequency limits the applicability of general word frequency counts to readability formulae which are to reflect potential difficulty of texts for particular groups rather than individuals.

The ease with which we can read a word depends not only upon its frequency in print but also upon the range of vocabulary which the reader possesses. When the reader has a wide range of words in his memory to choose from, he must read more of a word in order to know which it is. His skill in making the right response, of course, is based not only upon the reading of the single word, but also upon the response to other cues in the text. If this were not so, we would have the paradoxical position that people with a rich vocabulary would be slow readers since they would have to refer to very long lists before being able to pick out the correct word!

4 READING WORDS IN SEQUENCE

However intricate and interesting the study of single words might be, it does not take us very far in our understanding of language. As we do not string words together in a random order, we must seek to explain how the words come to be arranged as they are. We can understand one influence upon the grouping of words by looking at the way in which they occur together in speech. If we are presented with the word 'of' and are asked to suggest what word might follow, some words such as 'course' or 'the' are more likely to be put forward than 'at' or 'shouted'. Our selection of a word to follow the stimulus word is influenced by the frequency with which these words occur together in speech. This phenomenon, called collocation, plays a significant part in the sequencing of words.

Miller (1951) has studied systematically the effect of altering the probability of occurrence of words. He constructed texts based on what he called increasing 'approximations to English' and found that increasing the degree of approximation to normal English usage had a marked effect on reading performance. To understand the effect which sequencing of words may have on reading fluency, let us look more closely at collocation and 'successive approximations' in different passages.

Miller constructed a series of texts based upon this probability of co-occurrence of words in normal English prose. The examples quoted below are all taken from his text. In the first example, the words were simply chosen at random from a dictionary:

Zero order: combat callous irritability migrates depraved temporal prolix alas pillory nautical.

In the second example words were chosen at random from a prose text, so that frequency of occurrence is reflected in the selection:

First order: Day to is for they have proposed I the it materials of are its go studies the hour of the following.

In this case some words occur together by chance just as they would in normal prose; 'they' and 'have' go together frequently as do 'hour' and 'of'.

The next example reflects this tendency for words to collocate in pairs in normal prose; having been expressly selected on that basis:

Second order: Goes down here are not large feet are the happy days and so what is dead weight that many were constructed.

Clearly, texts may be constructed in which each word reflects the probability of its following any number of words. As the number of words used increases so the resulting sequences will approximate more and more closely to normal English prose. For example, taking account of the three previous words would produce sequences such as the following:

Fourth order: We are going to see him is not to chuckle loudly and depart for home.

We can see how collocation will affect the strings of words which we produce in a powerful way. Before speaking, we usually have a very general plan or an idea of what we want to say even though the specific words have not been chosen. However, when we begin to speak we find that the choice of words is being influenced by the preceding sequence. Sometimes, indeed, a situation may be reached where the listener gains an impression that a speaker is no longer in control of his language, rather the language seems to be controlling the speaker!

It has been found that increasing the degree of approximation to English leads to a tendency to improvement in certain tasks related to reading, such as reading aloud, recalling after a lapse of time, learning and typing. This improvement occurs, in fact, because the strings of words approximate more and more closely to the word sequences with which the individual reader is familiar. The readability of the text, therefore, will depend, to a significant extent, on the relationship between the sequences it contains and their familiarity to the individual reader. What is readable for a child with one sort of linguistic background may not be readable for a child whose linguistic background is very different. This is very clearly demonstrated in an experiment by Ruddell (1965).

Chapter 6   Sentences and Readability

We have seen that the sounds which we use in our language are restricted and that the way we use them is governed by rules or conventions. When we come to examine sentences, we find that there are certain rules which determine how words may be strung together. These are not statistical rules or probabilities such as we examined in the previous chapter. They are conventions which must be properly learned and applied if what we speak or write is to be regarded by others as correct English. This set of rules does not, of course, tell us what we must do—only what we may or may not do. Statistical probabilities can, in fact, be calculated to show the frequency of co-occurrence of different parts of speech, e.g. adjective and noun, or adjective and adjective. These probabilities, as we shall see later, provide a means of assessing differences between texts which in turn affect readability. These rules are most commonly referred to as the 'grammar' or 'syntax' of the language.

1   CATEGORIES IN SENTENCE ANALYSIS

In dealing with long sequences of words, we are seeking to describe the way in which some strings of words are regarded by speakers and listeners as more 'acceptable' than others. 'Fred hit the ball' is more acceptable than 'The hit Fred ball'. These acceptable sequences occur in what are termed constructions. We may think of them as 'compartments' into which words can be slotted. The compartments are very rigid however and only accept certain types of material. Note the following construction:

He sang.

We can see how 'he' in this construction could be replaced by any number of alternative subjects, such as 'The blackbird' or 'The stout over-dressed tenor' and the sentence would still be acceptable. Similarly, 'sang' could be replaced by a variety of alternative verbs, such as 'went out' or 'complained that he had been wronged'. In neither case is the basic construction affected even though some of the alternatives which may be submitted are long. Our knowledge of these categories within sentences leads us to recognise 'Strange evenings drink' as a similar admissible construction though the 'sense' or meaning of the sentence is hard to establish. 'You swine!' however, though superficially similar, does not belong to this category, being an exclamation, and so we cannot undertake the substitutions which were possible with 'He sang'. Yet again 'They very', though apparently similar, cannot be placed into any category. As it stands, it is an unacceptable construction, though the occurrence of the two words together would be acceptable in a sentence such as 'They very soon found otherwise'.

It may be seen from these examples that our understanding of a sentence will depend not only upon our knowledge of the words and the sequence but also upon our knowledge of the categories into which words can be placed, and the relationship which these categories have one to another. Indeed our understanding of any group of words will depend upon our ability to organise the group into some sort of structure.

In this description of language, the classes of things which go into the compartments must be clearly identified. They are referred to as form-classes, though many of them correspond to what have been traditionally called parts of speech. Carroll (1964 p. 92) gives six major form-classes (Nominals, Adjectivals, Verbals, Adverbials, Prepositionals, Conjunctives). These categories very nearly accommodate all the forms of language likely to be experienced and acquired by English speakers.

Carroll points out that many of these concepts of language are learned without the learner being aware of them. Among the very young children who are fluent speakers, it is safe to say that few, if any, will have learned to structure their speech as a result of receiving direct instruction in grammar! Indeed, even though the form-classes refer to certain common kinds of experiences, many people are scarcely aware of these classes. Yet the ability to respond consciously to these forms can in some cases be of assistance in understanding the ideas in speech or writing. For example, the phrase 'the more the merrier' carries in it the concept of correlation. Thus reference to the linguistic construction and its meaning may be used to help a student to grasp the statistical concept of correlation.

As far as the teacher is concerned, form-classes are a simple means of sorting different parts of a sentence in a way which may help children to understand the relationships between the parts without having to previously learn complicated rules and systems of analysis. Recent systems of categorising language in this way have provided a simple and useful means of analysing children's speech and examining its relationship to the language of books (see Loban 1963 and Strickland 1962).

If we regard the constructions of language as a set of categories in this way, then our analysis of the linguistic ability of an individual may be based upon the number of constructions which he has acquired and the number of form-classes which he can use and respond to. It has been demonstrated by Ruddell (1965) that this ability will in turn affect his approach to the constructions and form-classes encountered in print. He found that children's comprehension scores were significantly greater when the material used contained language structures which were highly frequent in speech than when materials contained structure patterns which were infrequent in speech. He concluded that reading comprehension is a function of the similarity of language patterns used in speech and those encountered in reading material. Measures of readability will therefore reflect, among other things, the relationship between oral and written language structures. A further gain for the teacher is that this type of analysis provides a simple but effective means of showing children the way in which sentences hold together, and the ways in which sentences can be rearranged to develop meaning.

While this description is useful, it still does not deal adequately with the relationships between the various words in a sentence. It will be helpful therefore to look at another system for describing language. The traditional method of describing the grammar of a sentence by 'parsing' has in recent years been replaced by methods which take into account ideas of how a sentence is produced in speech and also ideas from psychological studies of language.

2 STRUCTURE IN SENTENCES

Consider this example of a very familiar type of ambiguous sentence: 'They are eating apples.' We cannot establish its meaning until we know something about its structure, but this information can only be obtained by looking at a wider context. The example should really be regarded as two sentences which could be given in answer to two separate questions. One might be given in response to a question such as 'What are the children doing?' whereas the other question might be 'Are those apples for

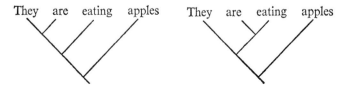

cooking or eating?' The ambiguity arises out of using one string of words to express two different constructions. We can easily see the structural difference between the alternative sentences if they are diagrammed as shown on p. 65.

This visual representation of the structure of sentences can be very helpful in measuring the complexity of language. The varying systems of visual representation of this kind reflect the ideas which modern linguists have about the way we speak in sentences, and one of these, utilised in assessing readability, is described below.

Yngve (1960) has proposed a model to explain how sentences are produced in this way. Before describing the model and its application to readability, it is necessary to outline the main observations and assumptions which are reflected in the construction of the model. When we are about to speak we usually have a plan or idea, albeit a subconscious one, about what we want to say. This idea is broken down into smaller pieces in accordance with the grammatical rules we have acquired until we produce the string of words which convey what we want to say.

The first assumption is that there is no natural limit to the length of sentences we can produce and very rarely does a speaker have a fully formed sentence worked out before he utters the first word. We often hear a speaker hesitate, become confused, and start again as he attempts to reorganise his sentence even as he is speaking it.

Secondly, it is important to remember that the words in a sentence are produced in a time sequence, which our orthography reflects in a left to right sequence in space. Thirdly, that a speaker's memory capacity for dealing with the production of speech is limited. Fourthly it is assumed that the production of a sentence is essentially a matter of expanding constructions. Every construction is expanded in turn into two other constructions or filled in with words.

Consider the sentence, 'He shouted'. This consists of a noun phrase (He) and a verb phrase (shouted) neither of which is expanded. The two branches of the sentence represent what are usually called the subject and predicate. When we consider the sentence 'The boy shouted' we can see that the sentence still consists of a noun phrase (The boy) and verb phrase (shouted). However, the noun phrase or left hand branch of the sentence has been expanded into a construction involving an article (The) and noun (boy), producing a slightly more complex sentence. When represented diagrammatically the two sentences would look like this:

He   shouted   The   boy   shouted

The following examples show both left hand and right hand expansions. In speech, since the sentence is in a time sequence, the left hand parts must be expanded first. Yngve points out that as the left hand parts of a sentence are expanded so the right hand parts of the sentence are delayed. The strain upon the memory of both speaker and listener is consequently increased. He suggests that the number of left handed expansions is usually limited by the human memory storage capacity. The amount of memory storage required to produce a sentence is called the 'depth' of the sentence and, as will be seen, can be quantified by means of a simple counting system. In general, the greater the depth of a sentence the more difficult it will be to understand. For example, the reader should find the phrase in the figure below on the left easier to read and understand than the phrase on the right.

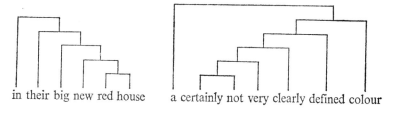

in their big new red house   a certainly not very clearly defined colour

The importance of this model within the context of readability lies in the fact that it offers a means of assessing the complexity of sentences, particularly in a way which can be expressed numerically. The counting scheme devised by Yngve is based on the number of words required in order to complete the word sequence grammatically. It is best explained by the example below:

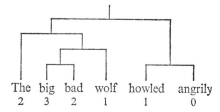

The   big   bad   wolf   howled   angrily
2   3   2   1   1   0

Thus, in the example above the word 'The' carries a value of two because the speaker must remember two structures to complete the sentence (a noun and a predicate). The word 'big' on the other hand has a depth of three because the speaker must produce an adjective, noun and predicate to complete the sentence. The total depth of this sentence is nine, and the average word depth 1·5.

An increase in the number of left hand expansions leads to an increase in the complexity of the sentence and this is reflected in the depth of the sentence when calculated in this way. This concept of word depth has been applied to the assessment of readability. Its value is discussed in greater detail in Chapter 8.

The response to sentence structure is likely to play an important part in determining readability since the acquisition and use of syntax is so significant in the development of language in children. Brown and Bellugi (1964), for example, have shown three stages in the child's acquisition of syntax. They point out that understanding sentence structures is the third stage and the one which the children in the sample found most difficult.

In addition to the use which we make of syntax in understanding words in sentences, we also use the meaning which we can extract from the words in the sequence. Consider the following example:

Yesterday, Tom Smith went to Swenby by
Yesterday, Ranji went to the jungle clearing by
(After Merritt 1970)

From the previous discussion it will be clear that the alternatives which are proposed for the missing word will be very much restricted by the influence of collocation and grammatical class. For example, non-nouns are unlikely to be proposed, but the particular nouns suggested will refer to modes of transport which might be expected from clues as to cultural contexts. 'Tom Smith' and 'Swenby' conjure up notions of Anglo Saxon origins and English towns or villages and so might lead to suggestions such as 'car' or 'bus' whereas the expectancies in the second sentence are in quite a different area although perhaps still related to transport. As Merritt explains, a person's fluency in reading will be influenced by his response to sequences of meanings as well as the linguistic factors described earlier, and so will affect readability. Thus, the readability of a text may be affected by the degree of correspondence between the experience and thoughts recorded in the texts and the experiences and thoughts of a reader.

Although in this analysis we have been very concerned with constructions which were acceptable, i.e. those which had an acceptable grammatical structure, there are many expressions which play an important part in speech, but which do not form sentences. These require some attention, since they are commonly encountered in reading.

In conversation we often use expressions such as 'Hello', 'Hey', 'Well' and 'm-hm' or 'O.K.'. The first example is a greeting. The second and third are used to attract attention and to signal that we are about to speak. The last two are responses to another speaker used to indicate that we are still listening or that we have heard and understood what was said. These 'nonsentential' expressions are frequent in speech and play an important part in conversation. We can see that they have a psychological rather than a grammatical function. We find these expressions much less frequently in writing than in speech. A writer must use other psychological and linguistic tricks to attract and hold the attention of the reader.

3 READING SENTENCES

It would be very convenient if we could work out the meaning of a sentence by adding up the meanings of the words considered separately. This is unfortunately not possible because, as we have seen, the way in which words interact prevents us from doing this. Whereas the sequence of words rarely affects a sentence in Latin, for example, the linear sequence of words in speech patterns in English is extremely important. For example, a 'Venetian blind' does not mean the same as a 'blind Venetian'. The linear arrangement of the words 'Venetian' and 'blind' has a profound effect upon the meaning of the two whether we consider them as separate words or as a phrase. Our ability to extract meaning from the phrase is closely related to the grammatical structure underlying it. Indeed, if we look again at the earlier example, 'They are eating apples', we can see that meaning of the sentence cannot be understood until we have established just what is the structure of the sentence. We can see from this type of example just how significant a part our response to the structures of language plays in understanding sentences.

In a series of experiments reported by Miller (1951) it was found that words were perceived much more easily when they were presented within the context of a sentence than when they were presented singly in a list of words, even though words spoken in sentences are often slurred and mispronounced. Miller has suggested that the principal unit of speech perception is not a single word or morpheme, but larger syntactic units. It is from these larger units that we obtain most of our meaning. If we were to print our language so that it reflects the most meaningful units of speech   thenapageofprintwouldprobablylook   somethinglikethis. As many teachers know from experience, children occasionally run words together in this way because they are not aware of the discrepancy between language units in speech and language units in writing.

The influence of the syntactic structure independent of meaningfulness and word co-occurrence was studied by Epstein (1961). Using nonsense syllables but adding grammatical tags, e.g. -ly, -ing, -s, and two words which have not denotative meaning, i.e. 'the' and 'in', he constructed 'sentences' such as:

i The yigs wur vumly rixing hum in yegest miv.
ii Yigs rixing wur miv hum vumly the in yegest.

In his experiment, Epstein found that subjects took significantly less time to learn sentences of the first type than they did sentences of the second type. This and related experiments indicate that the ability to respond to syntactic sequences is an important aid to learning. It seems very likely that the fluent reading of such material will similarly be assisted if the reader is able to respond to syntactic cues in this way.

In this context, Merritt's article (1970), contains a useful summary of the interaction of these different factors. After describing the skills which he classifies as intermediate, he goes on to argue that fluency is based upon the ability to respond simultaneously to the different kinds of sequence noted above. Merritt explains how the interaction of responses of this kind helps a reader to overcome problems of word recognition by reducing the number of possibilities against which the word causing difficulty has to be matched. The part which intermediate skills play in reading is described in too much detail to be properly condensed here. It is enough to say that clear indications of links between the development of intermediate skills and readability can be drawn out from Merritt's evidence. Some of the speculations provide many openings for useful research into the relationship between reading skills and the readability of texts differing in difficulty, as well as to activities which teachers could undertake in order to develop fluency.

Few studies seem to have systematically examined the relationship between children's language and the language structures of reading schemes. One study by Strickland (1962), however, set out to classify children's speech patterns into units and compare the occurrence of these linguistic patterns with those in selected reading texts. In the first stage of her investigation dealing with the spoken language of children, she suggested that six generalisations were warranted. Some expected findings were that although a wide range of language patterns was used by children of all ages, certain patterns such as subject—verb, subject—verb—direct-object, were used more frequently and appeared to be basic building blocks of their language. Also, significant differences in the use of movable phrases and clauses and patterns of subordination were found between children of different mental ages, parental occupational status and parental education.

When reading material was examined, only one of the basic sentence patterns used by children, namely the subject—verb—object pattern, appeared in practically all of the books. Further, the patterns of sentences used differed from book to book within a series as well as from series to series. These patterns appeared to be introduced, and, once introduced, they were not found to be followed by any sort of systematic repetition. Strickland's final conclusion was that there seemed to be no scheme for the control and development of sentence structures in reading materials which parallels the generally accepted control and development of vocabulary.

In this country, Reid (1970) has studied the same problem in relation to four reading schemes. She also concludes that discrepancies between the frequencies of sentence patterns in speech and print may influence reading difficulty and that this aspect of sentence structure should be investigated further. It is hoped that the observations of such researchers as Reid and Strickland will lead to an improvement in the control of sentence structure in material written for children.

Chapter 7   Beyond the Sentence

As we extract meaning from phrases and sentences which we hear, so we also extract meaning from longer sequences of sound, such as long conversations, news bulletins on radio or television, speeches and lectures. Although the sentence is conventionally the largest unit for syntactic analysis and description, in semantics we must consider the influence upon meaning when strings of sentences are put together.

1 LONG SPEECH UNITS

When we seek to understand long speeches, we do so by picking out main ideas and relationships which reflect the patterns of thought of the speakers. We listen for sentences which we think contain the important idea around which other related ideas are organised. Our ability to distinguish these main ideas will depend upon the density of ideas in the speech. The emphasis which the speaker gives to a sentence or its position in the sequence are also clues which we most frequently use in determining the significant parts of the speech.

A main idea in a passage is not always the most important thing to identify as, more often than not, there are several ideas which need to be identified and arranged in some sort of relationship. A number of common thought patterns have been described which, if responded to, considerably assist the listener in dealing with language.

Some common thought patterns are:

i Relationships involving a whole and its parts.
ii Relationship of cause and effect.
iii Relationships based upon a sequence (such as time or process).
iv Relationships based upon comparison and contrast.

As may be readily seen, our ability to respond to the thought patterns in speech is heavily dependent upon our own thinking. While our experience of language may help in the understanding of smaller speech units, it is our experience of different forms of thinking which affects the degree to which we can understand long utterances. As we shall see in the next section, our ability to analyse paragraphs is influenced by our knowledge of patterns of thought in our own language as well as in the language of an author.

2 READING LONG PASSAGES

Dealing with thought processes and the relationship between ideas in sentences is easier in print than in speech since the reader can scan the material again and again whereas the listener must rely heavily upon memory if he is to identify the train of thought of the speaker. The way in which we think and relate ideas together will influence our ability to understand the organisation of the paragraph.

As the four following examples from Niles (1963) indicate, the way in which the passage is ordered has a clear effect upon the meaning it conveys.

i 'During our visit to the museum, we saw a collection of old silverware, an absorbing display of old-fashioned wedding gowns, and a room filled with Indian relics, and the first Stars and Stripes ever carried in battle.'

This sentence is simply a list of objects and events with no stated relationship between the parts.

ii 'During our visit to the museum, we saw the first Stars and Stripes ever carried in battle; after that we enjoyed a collection of old silverware, later we wandered into the room filled with Indian relics, and finally found ourselves absorbed in a display of old wedding gowns.'

In this example, the ideas are related to one another and reflect a chronological sequence which corresponds to the sequence of rooms visited.

iii 'During our visit to the museum, we enjoyed seeing the first Stars and Stripes ever carried in battle and the absorbing display of old-fashioned wedding gowns much more than we did the room filled with Indian relics and the collection of old silverware.'

In this third example, the ideas are grouped into preferences and dislikes and the groups contrasted with one another. This contrast adds to the relationship within the sentence.

iv 'Because, on our visit to the museum, we had seen the first Stars and Stripes ever carried in battle, a room full of Indian relics, a display of old silverware, and a collection of old-fashioned wedding gowns, we were able to present a successful class program in which we compared relics of the past with their modern equivalents.'

The final example shows the same set of facts expressed in a cause-effect relationship. The ability to observe and use simple thought processes such as listing, sequencing, contrasting and comparing. and cause and effect relationships is one of the basic skills in comprehension. This ability is related not only to the linguistic skills of the reader but also his cognitive ability.

While the examples given are in fact sentences, it is clear that the understanding of paragraphs will be influenced by the reader's ability to perceive the same relationships when they are extended over several sentences. One simple and easily applied technique is described below.

The approach is based upon certain obvious techniques of precis, such as finding topic sentences and related ideas, but adds a new dimension to the exercise by representing paragraphs in visual form. This method for discovering and understanding the relationships between ideas within a paragraph has been suggested by Bissex, and is reported by Strang and Bracken, 1957. Bissex suggests further that it is helpful to visualise the organisation of a paragraph around the key or topic sentence, which must be identified.

He considers three theoretical forms of paragraph—inductive, deductive and balanced. Each form has four variations making a total of twelve visual patterns. As we might expect from our knowledge of the term 'inductive', the four varieties of this kind of paragraph follow a form in which a series of statements are given which culminate in a generalisation or wide conclusion. Thus the key or topic sentence is always at the end of the paragraph. Paragraphs which have a theoretically 'deductive' form, however, show the reverse pattern. As the examples below indicate, the key sentence, involving a major assumption, statement or generalisation, is given first and is then followed by a series of sentences which support or prove the generalisation. Finally, balanced paragraphs are constructed so that either two ideas are balanced around a key sentence in the middle, or, so that there are two key sentences, one at the beginning, the other at the end of the paragraph. Although the names given by Bissex to the twelve types of paragraph suggest a light hearted approach, the exercise of visualising paragraphs in this way may have some value in predicting the difficulty of texts. Bissex does not offer this as scientific evidence about paragraphs, but he does suggest that it might be a useful system for understanding texts and in addition increasing the effectiveness of writers.

The twelve types of paragraph, as visualised by Bissex, are given below, with a brief description of their main characteristics.

74

The four types of inductive paragraph are: *i.* the fable, *ii.* the salestalk, *iii.* the therefore, and *iv.* the receder.

i. The Fable

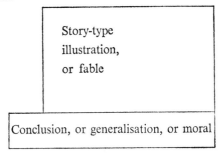

An anecdote or story-type illustration is followed by a generalisation stating, or implying the significance of the illustration.

ii. The Salestalk

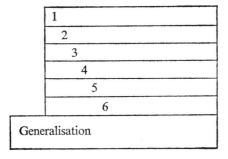

This type represents a list of items of any sort, e.g. causes, effects, implications, or facts, which is followed by an embracing or organising sentence. The order of items is not critical, and the success of paragraph depends upon a cumulative effect.

iii. The Therefore

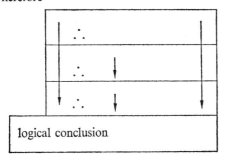

This pattern is similar to the salestalk, except that the statements are logically progressive, and a grand conclusion follows the chain of logic.

iv. The Receder

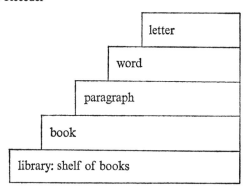

This type is similar to type *ii*, except that the paragraph has a sequence, e.g. from particular to general, minor to major, least important to most important.

The four forms of deductive paragraph proposed by Bissex are: *v.* the for example, *vi.* the count them, *vii.* the because, and *viii.* the advancer.

v. The For Example

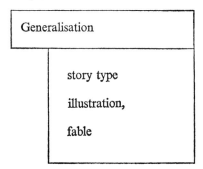

This is the opposite, in form, of type *i*. A generalisation is given, which is then followed by story, or anecdote, by way of illustration.

76

vi. The Count Them

Generalisation	
series of facts	1
names, or	2
examples	3
etc.	4
	5
	6

In this type, an assertion or generalisation is made, and a series of facts and other items are listed. The reader's idea about the truth of the assertion must grow as he reads.

vii. The Because

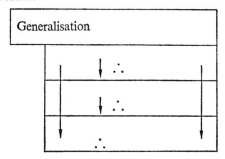

This type is a pure form of deduction and is the contrast of type *iii.* the therefore. A main generalisation is followed by a chain of logical steps. The generalisation is not repeated, and so the reader must remember the initial assertion as he proceeds through the paragraph.

viii. The Advancer

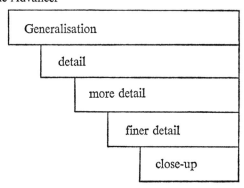

As this type is the contrast to type *iv*, the advancer moves, for example, from the general to the particular, from major to minor, or from distant to near-at-hand. Bissex suggests that this type is appropriate to physical description.

The third of the theoretical forms of paragraph, the balanced, is represented by *ix*. the come-on, *x*. the switch, *xi*. the classic, and *xii*. the thinker.

ix. The Come-on

This form begins with details or some attention-getter. The main generalisation is then given after which the paragraph is filled with more detail and trivia. The relationship, if any, between the detail and the main assertion, need not be clearly indicated.

x. The Switch

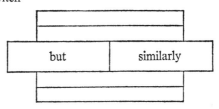

Here the reader must perceive similarities or differences. Key words such as 'similarly' or 'in the same way' indicate a move from less important ideas to the real substance of the passage. Words such as 'but' and 'on the other hand' usually signal the shift to the important ideas in a paragraph of contrast.

xi. The Classic

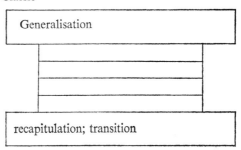

Here, a generalisation is given. Then there is a middle section or development, followed by a final recapitulating or reinforcing statement to conclude the paragraph.

xii. The Thinker.

```
┌─────────────────────────────┐
│  Main idea implied or       │
│                             │
│  stated elsewhere           │
│                             │
│                             │
│                             │
└─────────────────────────────┘
```

In this case, no generalisation is stated. The generalisation has to be found elsewhere, or very often, inferred by the reader.

Bissex found, unfortunately, that paragraphs do not always fall into these principal theoretical forms, and that many paragraphs are too short to be profitably categorised. The question arises, therefore, as to whether or not there is a relationship between the structure of the paragraph and its readability. This would seem to be a profitable area for small scale research, and should prove of value in improving reading comprehension, even if it does not turn out to be a system of analysis which can be incorporated into measures of readability. It would seem particularly valuable to people concerned with improving communication with those already fluent in reading.

SUMMARY

In Part 2 we have considered a series of factors in both the reader and the type which influence the extent to which a person will find a book readable. At each stage, important characteristics of the reader were described and their effects upon reading ability were discussed. The three major aspects of the reader to be considered were his interests and motivation, his ability to see the print, and his language. It was suggested that the relationship between interest and motivation and reading, though difficult to describe and evaluate, is of fundamental importance in the study of reading generally, but particularly in the study of readability.

In the field of legibility, certain factors in the print were shown to have a marked effect upon visibility and thus readability. The significance of the existence of 'optimal' conditions for reading print was discussed as were suggestions for the modification of type faces in ways which might lead to improved legibility. The relationship between spoken language and its visual form was considered. Factors involved at the level of sounds, words, sentences and paragraphs were described and the part which they play in reading was examined. It was established that a number of aspects of language combine and interact to have a marked effect upon readability.

The description of these determinants of readability has shown that many factors which affect readability can be clearly identified and in many cases controlled. The following chapter takes up the problem of measuring these factors and interactions so that by appropriate matching of individuals and books we can ensure more effective and pleasurable reading.

Part III   The Measurement of Readability

Chapter 8 Methods of Assessment

We have seen in the preceding pages that readability involves the interaction of many aspects of a reader and the books he reads. Though the earlier discussion of these factors may further our understanding of the way in which they influence one another, we must also review attempts to measure the way in which these factors interact. As was pointed out, there have been many attempts to assess the readability of books, using a variety of techniques. In this part of the study, several methods currently in use will be considered and specific examples described and discussed. Alternative approaches, arising from our increasing knowledge of how we read, will also be referred to.

1 METHODS OF MEASUREMENT

The methods which have been most commonly adopted may conveniently be arranged in five subsections and are described and discussed in the following order:

i subjective assessment
ii objective question and answer techniques
iii formulae
iv tables and charts
v sentence completion and cloze procedure.

The various measures to be looked at in each of these subsections reflect in some way the definitions of readability which were considered in part one. In that discussion, three main ideas, incorporated in the definitions were isolated. Readability was seen to involve (i) ease of reading, (ii) interest or compellingness, and (iii) ease of understanding. Most researchers have seemed to regard these three aspects as alternatives and as a result each measure devised reflects only one of them. It is perhaps useful to see what is being measured in each case.

Firstly, when referring to ease of reading, readability has come to be measured by use of word recognition speed, error rates, number of eye fixations per second and so on, all of which relate to primary skills and are measures of visibility or legibility. Secondly, when defined as interest or compellingness, readability has been measured by reference to human interest, density of ideas, and aesthetic judgements of style. Thirdly, when defined as ease of understanding or comprehension, measures have referred to characteristics of words and sentences, such as their length or frequency of occurrence, in the case of the former, and length and complexity in the case of the latter. Of these three alternatives, the third has been most frequently adopted, since for theoretical, technical and practical reasons, it presents fewer problems and offers greater possibilities for wide and frequent usage. Such measures do not, of course, measure all the ingredients essential to comprehension, as they give no indication of content or clarity of expression. There is, however, a technique for assessing readability which includes the reader. This provides a global measure to which all readability variables contribute.

It is unfortunate that studies of these various alternatives have all been grouped together under the heading of readability as if they were all dealing with the same issues. In the previous paragraph it has been shown that the alternatives are essentially different, reflecting as they do different reading skills. Thus, while speed of word recognition is an element affecting ease of understanding, a readability measure using the former cannot be equated with a readability measure involving comprehension. The criteria used in defining readability then are, regrettably, not comparable and, as will be seen, neither are the methods of measurement. The potential user must, therefore, know clearly what it is he wants to measure, whether a single aspect or the interaction of one or more variables. He must also know sufficient about the validity, reliability and adequacy of sampling of the measures from which he intends to make a selection. A detailed discussion of validity and sampling adequacy will be found in Klare (1963), chapters 7 and 8.

Whatever the distinctions between the alternatives may be, and whatever their implications for theorists, there remains a final general consideration which is of great importance to the teacher, librarian or reader. When assessing measures of readability, four points influence choice. The methods devised must be easy to apply, easy to mark, easy to calculate, and accurate. The necessity to take account of these factors which are extremely important to a teacher has proved a difficult problem for workers devising readability measures. Very often, the accuracy of a measure decreases with its ease of application. In such a situation it is difficult, if not impossible, to find a satisfactory balance between conflicting needs. Of course, for some research purposes ease of application and ease of marking may not be the prime considerations. A researcher may be quite happy to use a very detailed and laborious procedure if it suits his needs. A teacher on the other hand may not need quite such a refined procedure and will have little use for any procedure which is likely to take up a substantial amount of time.

i Subjective judgements

In the absence of convenient quantitative methods, most assessments of the readability of books have involved the use of a subjective judgement. The intending reader haphazardly casts a glance through the pages using such clues as content, style, range of vocabulary, format and organisation as a basis for judgement. Librarians, choosing on behalf of readers, are obliged to operate in this way, but may make more reliable judgements about the readability of texts in view of their training and wide experience of books. Unfortunately, they may have little precise information on the readers so they must indulge in some unreliable guesswork.

Teachers, like librarians, are required to choose books on behalf of others and they too are usually obliged to make highly subjective estimates. Their position may be slightly better than that of the librarian since they have a closer contact with the readers. Knowing more about their pupils' interests and capabilities, they may be more effective in their estimates of readability and their choices, as a result, may be consequently more accurate and appropriate. Chall (1958) reported that while teachers were consistent in their rankings of the difficulty of books, and while these rankings corresponded to objective measures of difficulty, their rankings of books and children were inaccurate and inadequate.

Studies of systems of marking examination papers have shown that the inadequacies of individual subjective judgements can in some way be improved upon by the use of groups of examiners. The use of combined judgements has also been tried in the assessment of readability. Moyle (1971) lists two studies involving the grading of books by committees of experienced teachers. The results of these studies show a pattern typical of assessment by panels—the grading done by the committees is much more consistent than that by individuals. This improvement in the consistency of judgements is only relative however, since the studies reported by Chall (1958) demonstrated the unreliability and inconsistency of even expert judgement.

Surveys of reading interests and the frequency of usage of books, such as that undertaken by Abernethy *et al.* (1967) and those reported by Chall, which essentially reflect the subjective judgement of the reader, offer broad frameworks within which to assess books. Such guide lines are crude and are of little use in estimating the readability of particular books, since judgements of the readers may be greatly affected by motivational influences referred to earlier and so lead to widely inconsistent gradings of texts. However, the facts gleaned from this type of survey, which could be undertaken by children, could be of use in organising library displays and determining general ranges of books. There is a need for many small, but detailed, studies of children's reading habits both in school and out. Using library cards, a census of 'book traffic' undertaken by children would provide useful information to the teacher and at the same time, as the results are tabulated, open up many opportunities to discuss the interest value of books, the style and their literary merit as seen by the children, and so on.

A recent attempt to assist librarians, teachers and readers in the selection of books was made by Kamm and Taylor (1966). They recognise the problem involved in selecting books for particular purposes and needs, when the choice available is vast and increasing every year. Their solution to the problem is to provide useful information on the preparation, publication and use of books and to offer opinions as to the suitability of various types of books for various readers and situations. While much of the book contains factual information, the advice is still essentially subjective and based upon the authors' assumptions and values. However, the attempted impartiality of this approach may well be more desirable and reliable than the publicity issued by publishers and authors concerning the appropriate readership of their texts. The survey described earlier by Clarke (1970) also contains some subjective evidence upon which to base judgements.

The continuing search for an adequate system to indicate the appropriate readership of children's books is reflected in a recent classification proposed by the Children's Book Group of the Publishers' Association. The 'Key System', as it is to be named, indicates the Reading Ability and Interest Age of a book. The classifications are arranged as follows:

Reading Age		Interest Age	
Under 6 yrs	1	Under 6 yrs	A
6 to 8 yrs	2	6 to 8 yrs	B
8 to 10 yrs	3	8 to 10 yrs	C
10+ yrs	4	10 to 12 yrs	D
		12+ yrs	E

Books may have only one Reading Ability classification but of course may cover several interest ages. For example, a book written for older children but which contains many illustrations might be given the classification 4 CDE.

The Key System may claim a number of advantages over the haphazard subjective classification of books. Firstly, it provides information in a standardised coded form which is easily understood. Secondly, if carefully applied, books from different publishers which are in many ways similar, are more likely to carry the same coding and may therefore be more readily compared. Thirdly, books for different purposes may be more easily distinguished. For example, the coding given would indicate books in which the content was intended to interest older children but which were written for retarded readers. Fourthly, a classification based on narrower age groups may be more helpful than such sweeping and ambiguous categories as 'and upwards' or 'lower Juniors' or 'Middle schools'. This simple coding system, if generally adopted by publishers, would help to rationalise the confusing state of affairs.

However, though the system attempts to bring some order into the assessment of readability, and though the system was apparently finalised only after many trials, it remains essentially a subjective system. The original classification does not seem to have been tested against objective measures of reading ability or interest. Also, publishers are expected to simply use their own judgement to assess within which of the four reading ability groups a particular book falls. While it improves upon the existing state of affairs, the Key System is still subject to the adverse comments which have been levelled at subjective measures of readability.

The unreliability of these subjective assessments and the increasing necessity for reliable and accessible measures has led to the utilisation of other methods more frequently employed for the conventional measurement of reading comprehension. In addition, it would seem obvious that such factors as ease of reading and familiarity of vocabulary could be more reliably assessed by looking at children's performances on different objective measures.

ii Question and answer techniques

Conventional question and answer techniques have frequently been employed, particularly to measure the difficulty of a passage, but also as a criterion against which other measures can be compared. This procedure, which is essentially measuring comprehension of content, while more impartial and controlled than subjective estimates, has several limitations which restrict its utility.

Firstly, it is impossible to ascertain whether a given response is a reflection of the complexity of the passage or merely a reflection of the difficulty of the question: for example, the content of a question may be simple, but complex phrasing may interfere with the reader's ability to provide the correct answer. Alternatively, the phrasing may be simple, but it may call for a very sophisticated interpretation of the text. Secondly, the response to questions occurring in the same order as ideas in the passage will differ from a response to a set of questions which have been given in random order. Thirdly, the conditions under which the questions are asked will affect the outcome: for example, the use of time restrictions has been found to adversely affect many people in test situations. Again, the retention or removal of the passage during questioning will affect the responses, since the reader has to rely upon memory to complete the questions. In many cases the marker may have to give a judgement about the suitability of the answer, so that the assessment is then contaminated by the subjectivity of the marker.

Objective questions of the multiple choice type have frequently been employed to test recall of content. These questions usually take a form in which the reader has to tick, cross or underline the correct item from a range of alternatives. While they have the advantage of being easily scored, they are restricted in their use since the responses have been found to be affected by the range and type of alternatives offered to the reader. Scores may be similarly affected by guessing. Furthermore, the proper preparation of multiple choice items requires a detailed knowledge of test construction and this is rarely possessed by the people interested in assessing readability. Multiple choice questions are affected by the ability of the reader to make an inspired guess based upon an imperfect understanding of content and provide a somewhat inadequate measure, therefore, of readability.

Requiring the reader to summarise or precis the text is a frequently used technique for assessing the level of understanding. However, it is an inadequate tool for use in readability studies, since the translation and production of a response include many skills which bear little or no relationship to those required in comprehension. In addition to these technical shortcomings, these methods assess only the extent to which the reader can pick out the content of the passage, they do not reflect the other components of readability, such as fluency, referred to earlier. A further difficulty in the use of precis as a measure of comprehension is that the precis must also be assessed subjectively by the marker. As we have seen, subjective assessment is highly unreliable and is quite inadequate for the purposes of providing a systematic and accurate measure of readability.

Though the above techniques are often used as measures of comprehension, they are of dubious value, in many cases, even for this purpose, and are quite unsuitable for use in readability. Researchers have sought other approaches to the problem.

iii Readability formulae

These are the most frequently produced and widely accepted methods for measuring readability, based as they are upon an analysis of easily identifiable aspects of the text. Each formula samples, in effect, one or more of the primary, intermediate or higher order reading skills which have been described in the preceding section of this study.

The application of a formula usually involves the selection of a sample from a text, the counting of some easily identifiable characteristics, such as the average number of words per sentence or the proportion of polysyllabic words in the sample, and then performing a calculation to produce a score. This score indicates the difficulty of the sample of text. If the sampling procedures advocated by the constructors are carefully followed, then it is assumed that this score reflects the difficulty of the whole text.

Many measures of this type have been put forward. They vary widely in the type and number of factors used and the size of samples required. Not all have been tested and validated systematically and not all have been accepted as genuine 'formulae'. Klare (1963), in a thorough survey of readability formulae, lists thirty-one established procedures, and admits that others exist which were not listed specifically. To this list must be added other formulae published since that date.

For the purpose of this study, it is not necessary to examine all the formulae published. Those to be discussed have been selected on the grounds that they are typical, popular, easy to apply, exemplify various factors frequently utilised, or have special application. It is hoped that all of them may prove helpful to those wishing to engage in the objective assessment of readability. For convenience, the formulae are presented in the order of their date of publication.

Morris and Halverson (1938) Idea Analysis Technique

A sample of text must be selected, and key words and phrases which convey ideas, referred to as 'content' words, are separated into four classifications as follows:

Classification I: the simplest word labels learned early in life common to all members of a given culture.

Classification II: words learned early in life but which are simple localisms used by groups within the population (e.g. corn and cattle in a rural area, tide and trawler in a fishing community).

Classification III: words referring to concrete ideas, e.g. persons' names, places, objects, processes, usually acquired through formal education and contact with 'educated' social groups.

Classification IV: abstract words referring to qualities, states of mind, and other referents which lack the tangibility of concrete word labels.

The authors formulated a wide number of rules for analysing texts by this method, though little information is provided on criteria, validity or applicability. These theoretical shortcomings, together with problems of time consuming administration and basic inaccessibility, have resulted in the formula being little used. The formula assesses readability of a passage by referring to the meaning of the 'content' words. In terms of the preceding analysis of language, this approach concentrates on the semantic aspect of words, though the classifications also reflect, indirectly, the statistical probabilities of the occurrence of words, and stages of verbal learning. The authors assume that a readability measure should reflect the understanding which the reader has of the text and this will depend upon the author's choice of words and the relationships between ideas. This does not allow for the fact that the ease or difficulty of a word will depend upon the context in which it is used.

This approach is early and outside the general trend of development. It is included because it exemplifies a systematic attempt to objectify and measure 'ideas' and their relationship to the meaning of the passages—a factor which until recently has received scant attention from later workers, even though all have recognised the importance of the meanings of words, and the need to measure the comprehension of the passage. The value of the formula is limited, however, because it reflects such a narrow range of the spectrum of skills which at different levels have been seen to affect readability.

Flesch (1948)

i. Reading Ease Formula. The instructions for using this formula are as follows:

To measure the readability of a passage, the following steps must be taken:

Systematically select 100 word samples from the text.
Determine the number of syllables per 100 words.
Determine the average number of words per sentence.
These two factors are represented by wl (word length) and sl (sentence length) respectively in the formula, given below.

Calculate the following equation:
Reading Ease $= 206 \cdot 835 - \cdot 846$ wl $- 1 \cdot 015$ sl.

Reading Ease represents the grade level which would have to be attained in order to read the passage.

ii. Human Interest Formula.
Select 100 word samples as above.
Count the number of personal words per 100 words (pw) in the formula.
Count the number of personal sentences per 100 sentences (ps) in the formula.
Calculate the equation:
Human Interest $= 3 \cdot 635$ pw $- \cdot 314$ ps.

This formulae emerged from an early measure which Flesch devised and has become one of the most widely known and frequently used of all formulae. The samples of text to be used are easily prepared though judgement as to the number of samples required is left to the user of the formula. The equation, by comparison to others, is relatively simple. The factors measured reflect aspects of the difficulty of reading single words and sentences. The word factor may be seen as a measure of semantic difficulty since syllable counts are a reflection of word length. The higher syllable counts will tend to measure rarity of words and therefore difficulty of meaning. The sentence measure used is a reflection of memory span, since the longer a sentence is, the more difficult it will be to remember the parts and so the more difficult it will be to understand. These points will be referred to in the general discussion which follows the description of other formulae.

It can be seen that this formula, incorporating as it does word and sentence measures, therefore reflects a wider range of linguistic skills than the previous formula. The skills reflected are within the primary and intermediate range. No attempt is made to assess directly the meanings of words or higher comprehension skills. However, the use of a measure of 'Human Interest' recognises the need to involve motivation and personal characteristics of the reader. The assumption that this is best done by measuring personal references has been shown to be reasonable, though its use has been criticised by Dale and Chall (1948), who argue that this measure could be misleading in some works where personal references are used as rhetorical and other literary devices.

In order to assess the potential of any formula, we need to know to what extent it is reliable, and to what extent it is measuring what we want it to measure. It is therefore necessary to examine the evidence of the validity of the formulae. Numerous validation studies involving the Flesch formulae are to be found (c.f. Klare 1963). These studies use different criteria, such as comprehension test scores, expert judgement and speed of reading; for example, Klare reported correlations between the Reading Ease formula and the Ojemann and Gray-Leary Reading Tests of ·82 and ·55 respectively. Klare also reported studies showing correlations with expert judgement ranging from ·61 to ·84. The highest correlation reported (·98) was between the Flesch and the Dale-Chall readability formulae. Most correlations are in the region of ·7. This seems to be the general level of correlation for most of the readability measures in use, though it has been argued by Bormuth (1966) that it might be possible to improve on these figures by the revision of formulae and a reappraisal of the factors used in calculation.

Dale and Chall (1948)

The instructions are as follows:
Select 100 word samples throughout the text (for books every tenth page is recommended).
Compute the average sentence length in words (x_2).
Compute the percentage of words outside the Dale list of 3,000 (x_1 or Dale score).
Calculate the equation:

$$Xc_{50} = ·1579x_1 + ·0496x_2 + 3·6365$$

where Xc_{50} is the reading grade score of a pupil who answers one half of a series of test questions (c) correctly.

The sentence factor used in the formula is the same as in the Flesch formula, and while the word factor appears to be different, it will be argued later that it is in effect measuring the same influence as the Flesch syllable count. Also the use of a word frequency list produces a similar effect to that of the Morris and Halverson word list. Classifications III and IV of their list would be more likely to contain content words outside the Dale-Chall list, while classifications I and II would contain more of the words included in that list.

This formula, which has proved as popular as the Flesch formula, is based on the assumption that only two factors, a word and a sentence factor, are necessary for the development of an efficient and reliable formula. The authors claim that a personal preference count is unnecessary and that reference to a large word list would prove a better predictor than the Dale 769 word list or a count of syllables. It is claimed to be efficient, but, if the recommended sampling procedure is followed, then very large numbers or words will need to be processed. Unfortunately, attempting to save time by reducing the sample size reduces the reliability of the results and the authors do not indicate what, in practical terms, would be the significance of reducing the sample size. The Dale-Chall formula, like the Flesch Reading Ease formula, reflects skills in the primary and intermediate range. There is no direct attempt to deal with familiarity and motivation, though the measure of word frequency will reflect the semantic load of the text.

As in the case of the Flesch formula, many validation studies have been reported, involving a variety of criteria. Klare (1963) reported correlations of ·87 and ·61 between the Dale-Chall formula and the Ojemann and the Gray-Leary Reading Tests. Dale and Chall themselves reported a correlation of ·90 between teachers' judgements of the difficulty of texts and the reading grade levels calculated from the formula. Similarly, a correlation of ·86 between judgements and formula was reported by Guckenheimer (1947). Of the formulae discussed in this section, validations of the Dale-Chall formula have produced the most consistent, as well as some of the highest, correlations.

Gunning (1952) The 'Fog Index'

The instructions for calculating this formula are as follows:
Select systematically samples of 100 words.
Determine the average sentence length: number of words divided by the number of sentences.
Determine the percentage of hard words by counting the number of words of three or more syllables (with some exceptions).
Obtain the Fog Index by totalling these two factors and multiplying by ·4.

The Fog Index gives the reading grade level required for understanding the material. This formula is clearly similar to that of Flesch. The factors remain the same but the counting of three syllable words will be easier and require less time than the syllable count required by Flesch. A further advantage lies in the simplicity of calculation required to resolve the equation. These two advantages of ease of application and calculation give the Fog Index a similar advantage over the Dale-Chall formula.

Only one correlation coefficient, of ·59, is quoted by Klare as validation of the Fog Index. Klare (1963) stated that in the case of this formula the usual procedure seemed to have been to make a rough comparison of results using the formula with some criterion, or to use some 'logical' basis for the assumption of validity.

McLaughlin (1969) SMOG Grading

This formula which is given the title of SMOG grading (Simple Measure of Gobbledygook) as a tribute to Gunning's Fog Index involves the following calculations:

Count 10 consecutive sentences near the beginning, 10 near the middle and 10 near the end of the text.

In the 30 selected sentences count every word of 3 or more syllables.

Estimate the square root of the number of polysyllabic words thus counted.

Add 3 to the approximate square root.

This gives the SMOG grade which is the reading grade that a person must have reached if he is to understand fully the text assessed. Though sentences are used to prepare a sample, they are not used in the calculation. As may be expected, it is claimed to be quick and easy to apply. Using a very small sample, this very recent formula is therefore predicting readability on the basis of one factor, namely, the word.

Thus, the range of skills directly assessed by the use of this formula is limited to those related to the identification and processing of words. Once again, the use of word length will involve, indirectly, differences in the semantic difficulty of the texts in a general way; a point which is returned to in a later discussion of formulae.

Validation studies are quoted to vindicate the two assumptions made; firstly, that counting polysyllabic words in a fixed number of sentences accurately reflects the relative difficulties of texts, and secondly, that the formula for converting the word counts into reading grades gives acceptable results.

A comparison of Dale-Chall and SMOG gradings showed that the SMOG gradings were generally two grades higher. This finding is accounted for by the fact that SMOG grades use a more severe criterion than the Dale-Chall formula; for McLaughlin used complete success as his criterion for comprehension while Dale and Chall accepted 50 per cent success as their criterion. For more detailed description and comment on these and other formulae, together with reports and discussions of validity, reliability studies and comparative surveys, Klare (1963) and Chall (1958) are recommended. With the exception of Morris and Halverson's study, this sample reflects certain points common to most other formulae, which limit their value as measures of readability.

To illustrate the effect of applying formulae to different texts, the last three formulae, Dale-Chall, Gunning and McLaughlin, have been applied to passages from two books, the Plowden Report and *The Valley of Adventure* by Enid Blyton. The results are as follows:

	Plowden Report	*Valley of Adventure*
Dale-Chall	13–15th Grade	7–8th Grade
Gunning	15th Grade	10th Grade
McLaughlin	13th Grade	8th Grade

It can be seen that in both cases the Gunning formulae produces higher results than the other two. This could be taken to indicate that the Dale-Chall and McLaughlin formulae are underestimating the difficulty of the texts or that Gunning's index is overestimating the difficulty. We could try to find out which was the more accurate by testing a sample of children using passages from the books and testing their comprehension of them in the conventional way. This would produce difficulties, as was mentioned earlier, and so it may be better to adopt a different form of assessment, namely the cloze procedure, which will be discussed later. Further difficulties in the way the results are expressed, the time taken to calculate, and so on, require more careful consideration.

Firstly, each formula requires the systematic selection of samples, varying in number and length. Consequently, these selection procedures vary in the amount of time required for completion. In view of the fact that saving time by altering the recommended sample sizes renders the measure unreliable, the teacher may prefer the SMOG index since groups of 10 sentences are easier to pick out than groups of 100 words. In addition, the teacher does not have to make a judgement as to how many samples he has to prepare.

It is yet too early to assess the acceptability, in practical terms, of McLaughlin's SMOG gradings, but he does claim that using his index, a reliable grading can be produced in only nine minutes. It should be pointed out, however, that ease of application is not of paramount importance. While, in general, it will affect the choice between formulae of similar validity, the needs of research or a particular application may demand the use of more complex and time consuming formulae. At a practical level, the related problems of excessive working time, difficulties in computation, and difficulties in making administrative judgements have led to a restriction of the use of many formulae to a narrow professionally interested group. Many teachers and librarians have been deterred by the additional work load even though the possible educational profit might have appeared attractive.

Also, regrettably, formulae rarely indicate the manner in which this result will be affected by variations in sample size. In general, the rule must be to adhere exactly to the sample requirements of the formula but in practical situations some knowledge of the degree of flexibility allowed in varying the number and size of samples required would be helpful in cutting down on work time.

Secondly, the formulae all involve the general use of a word measure and a sentence measure. This reflects the conclusion of researchers that reading difficulty is centred around factors at word and sentence levels. More recent work has suggested that this may be an oversimplification, but the practical value of using identifiable factors at these two levels makes them a very popular choice in the construction of formulae.

There is, however, a further problem. Both word length and sentence length can be unreliable as indices of readability. For example, despite its length the word 'grandfather' because of its familiarity will be more readable than 'sen' for the average reader yet in terms of word length and pronunciability, the latter would appear to be easier. Similarly, at the sentence level, a short sentence of unusual structure may be more difficult to read than a longer, more familiar structure. If sentençe length was a reliable measure, then sentence (*a*) below (15 words) should be more readable than sentence (*b*) (19 words). The reader must judge for himself whether or not this is so!

a What what what he wanted cost in Middle Wallop would buy in London was amazing (15 words)
b It was amazing what could be bought in Middle Wallop for the cost in London of what he wanted (19 words) (after Yngve 1960)

This comment should not be interpreted as a complete rejection of sentence length as a relevant factor in readability formulae. As longer sentences do tend to be more complex than shorter sentences, sentence length measures reflect the effect of memory span upon readability. Other measures are required, however, if the complexity of sentence structure is to be measured accurately.

Another criticism of this aspect of readability formulae is that, while the factors used in these formulae (over 150 have been counted) are easy to identify and count, they do not take into account motivational, situational or typographical factors, all of which have been shown to play an important part in determining the readability of a text.

A criticism which relates to the application of the formulae is that very few can be applied to the lower levels of reading ability and to basal reading schemes. Dolch (1948) and Spache (1953) have devised formulae with this area specifically in mind but these approaches suffer the criticisms which have been described earlier. Klare (1963) quotes reports which suggest that the Dale list of 769 most frequent words, used in the Spache formula, is inappropriate.

Yet another criticism deals with a basic assumption underlying readability formulae, and that is that the relationship between increasing word and sentence difficulty and reading ability is linear, that is to say that as words become more difficult, the reading ability required to cope with the increased difficulty will rise by an equal amount at every stage. If this relationship was linear it would be represented on the graph by the dotted line.

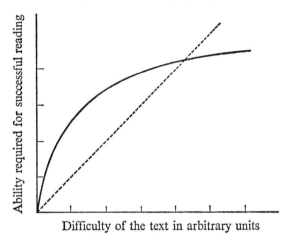

Difficulty of the text in arbitrary units

McLaughlin (1968) expounding this criticism states that this assumption is almost certainly false and that the difficulty of the text, however measured, will show a curvilinear relationship to reading age. When graphed, this relationship would follow a curved line, as shown above. This curvilinear relationship means that at the lower end of the reading ability range a small increase in difficulty will require a significant increase in reading skill if it is to be coped with. Further up the reading ability range, however, a significant increase in the difficulty of the text as measured by a formula requires only a small increase in reading skill if it is to be coped with.

Also a further basic assumption, reported to have been proved false as early as 1935 by Gray and Leary, is also questioned by McLaughlin. This assumption is 'that whatever the skill of the reader, the degree to which he is deterred by word difficulty compared with sentence difficulty remains constant' (McLaughlin 1968 p. 120). This statement implies that the reader's skill in dealing with increasingly difficult words rises in the same proportion as his skill in dealing with increasingly difficult sentences. However, as many teachers know, a poor reader may have such difficulty with word recognition that factors involved at the sentence level are irrelevant. A more competent reader, on the other hand, may generally find sentence structure more difficult than word recognition. These observations are, of course, related to the stages of development of the reading skills outlined earlier. The poor reader, having difficulty with word recognition, is showing weaknesses in the primary skills, whereas the more competent reader, while showing adequate primary skills, needs to develop intermediate and higher order skills if he is to improve his reading. Many teachers of reading may have noticed these phenomena, without perhaps formulating them in this manner, and have adapted their teaching to take account of the variations in difficulty and the different skills required. The clarification of this relationship by means of a series of readability studies would be of real value to the teacher, since it could provide a clearer understanding of the way in which the teaching of reading may help to overcome the difficulties involved.

Support for McLaughlin's criticisms comes from Bormuth (1966), who has provided evidence to show that the relationship between comprehension difficulty and linguistic variables in some cases is not linear and also that linguistic variables exert a different influence upon readers at different levels of ability. If we relate these findings to practical situations, it means that particular formulae may be appropriate only to a limited range of materials. Unless these limitations are known, the value of the formulae for teachers may well be lost. This criticism is disputed by some writers. Bormuth, for example, argues from the results of his study that a single readability formula can be used to predict difficulty for subjects at almost any level of reading ability.

A further criticism of formulae has been put forward by Taylor (1953). He maintains that formulae are particularly insensitive to the effects of textual factors upon specific individuals or small groups. Also, he argues that formulae are insensitive to the effect of previous knowledge of the book, and for the measurement of the readability of passages involving the non-idiomatic use of language and collections of words which have little meaning for an individual. These criticisms all reflect the point that, as they are conventionally used, readability formulae deal with only one side of the matching exercise, namely the book. The teacher requires measures which may also reflect factors in the reader which are influencing readability.

The reader will have noticed that the level of difficulty of a passage is expressed as a Reading Grade. A practical problem which must be overcome if formulae are to be used in this country involves the selection of an alternative method of representing the difficulty of texts. The use of Reading Ages derived from standardised reading tests, measuring word recognition and comprehension, seems an obvious way to express the levels of difficulty of the texts but the use of standardised cloze tests (see below) may, it will be argued, provide a more suitable alternative. The development of such a battery of standardised tests graded in difficulty would prove as useful to researchers and teachers in this country as the McCall-Crabbs Standard Test lessons (a series of passages carefully graded in increasing order of difficulty) have proved in the U.S.A.

Formulae were the earliest and most widely developed objective measures. The greater attention paid to this method of assessing readability is a reflection of the amount of information available on it, and the detailed comment a reflection of the intensity with which it has been studied. Attempts to overcome the criticisms outlined above have led not only to a search for new factors and more refined formulae but also to the development of completely different methods of assessing readability.

4 GRAPHS AND CHARTS

The use of graphs and charts is advocated in an attempt to facilitate the assessment of readability. The case for the use of tables for predicting readability is receiving increasing attention although few tables and graphs have, as yet, been produced. As will be seen, it is still necessary to select samples from texts and to count the incidence of one or more factors. They have the advantage of requiring little or no calculation since the results are related to a set of previously prepared tables. They are an easier and more familiar technique for preparing and evaluating data than formulae.

Fry (1968) describes a formula which was developed for use in Uganda and which he claims is quick and simple to use. Three one-hundred-word passages are selected and the total number of sentences in each is counted and the average of these three numbers is taken. Next the number of syllables in each one-hundred-word sample is counted and also averaged. These two averages are then plotted on a graph provided by Fry (see below) to give the appropriate grade level.

Graph for estimating readability by Edward Fry, Rutgers University Reading Centre.

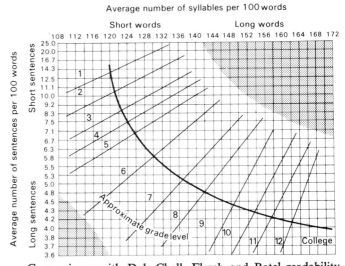

Comparisons with Dale-Chall, Flesch and Botel readability formulae produced high correlations (·94, ·96 and ·78 respectively) and led Fry to conclude that the Readability Graph is equally reliable but has the distinct advantage of requiring no mathematical calculations. As in the case of the formulae discussed earlier, the use of reading grades is inappropriate for this country but the idea might well be developed since it offers a means of assessing readability which is easy to operate and by which the results can be deduced from a table which is easy to understand.

Mugford (1969) describes a new Readability Chart which he has devised. The use of the chart depends on the allocation of points to words in different categories. These categories are based upon the numbers of polysyllabic words and the number of letters in words. The total number of points obtained for one-hundred-word samples from the text is converted into a reading age level by means of a table. As in the case of Fry's procedure, this idea has the advantage of requiring no computation other than counting, and judgements as to the scoring of words may be easily made. Unfortunately, no details of validation and reliability studies are available, but they are necessary before the procedure can be properly compared with other measures.

McLeod (1962) also described a method for the assessment of readability of books of low difficulty. This study is of interest, not only as an example of a type of readability table, but also as an all too rare attempt to estimate the readability of elementary reading books for young children, and those with poorly developed reading skills. For this reason, the article should be of particular interest to teachers involved in the teaching of reading in the early stages.

Using tests of word recognition and comprehension, McLeod assessed the performance of some 200 children and matched the reading scores to their ability to read passages from four books of a reading scheme. The results are presented in two tables. The first indicates the proportion of children successfully reading a given passage, according to reading age, and the second indicates the proportion successfully answering comprehension questions from a given book. The distribution of these proportions reflects the increasing levels of difficulty of the reading books. The reading age can be used as a predictor of likely success with a given book within the series tested. Though prediction of readability is restricted to the books which were used in the study, the technique is adaptable and can be used in connection with other reading materials.

McLaughlin (1968) proposed a readability table which could be prepared in the following way. A large sample of children would be asked to list any books which they had read and enjoyed during the previous three months. These lists would then be compared with a list of 240 books, composed of six groups with 40 books in each, which librarians find to be most often borrowed by children in six age groups, which are 6 and below, 7 to 8, 9 to 10, 11 to 12, 13 to 14, 15 and above. The teachers would then write against each book on the librarians' list the ages of any children who claim to have read and enjoyed it. The 240 books would then be analysed for word and sentence length and the data computerised to produce a readability table. The suggestion is based on a number of assumptions, outlined by McLaughlin, about the factors which are useful in measuring readability, the theoretical models for word and sentence comprehension, and the interaction between word and sentence factors.

This idea is useful in that the readers' interests are incorporated into the assessment of readability, though this may lead to a restriction in the range of reading materials assessed and, consequently, lead to a limitation in the applicability of the table. The preparation of such a table would involve a large scale research and it seems unlikely that the scheme, as suggested, will be undertaken. While the prospect of being able to predict levels of difficulty from a table seems attractive, it is possible that the teacher will find the proposals of other authors referred to of more immediate value. Also, it is argued that other bases for

101

constructing a readability table may be used which deal with the problem of measuring readability and, in addition, have value as a teaching aid.

5 SENTENCE COMPLETION AND CLOZE PROCEDURE

Like the question and answer techniques already referred to, sentence completion exercises are a familiar and long established means of assessing comprehension. Sentences are taken from the passage and certain words omitted. The degree of comprehension is the extent to which a person who has read the passage can replace the omissions correctly. The words to be replaced have usually been chosen to reflect only the content of the passage and often have little or no connection with linguistic complexity.

The principle has been amended by Taylor (1953), and under the title of *Cloze Procedure* it is being used as a measure of readability itself. The use of the cloze procedure involves the deletion of a number of words randomly determined or at fixed intervals, commonly every fifth word. Subjects are then asked to complete the passages and the number of correct responses is scored. In contrasting passages, those on which higher scores were obtained will be regarded as more readable than those on which lower scores were obtained.

The term 'cloze' derives from the Gestalt term 'clozure'. It is used to describe the tendency for a person mentally to complete or make whole an incomplete pattern and to see complete patterns as figures more readily than incomplete ones. Humans are similarly able to fill in gaps in spoken or written sentences and will tend to do so. Taylor defines a cloze unit as 'any single occurrence of a successful attempt to reproduce accurately a part deleted from a "message" by deciding from the context that remains what the missing part should be'.

Although different proportions of words were deleted by Taylor he reported that deletions of between 10 per cent and 20 per cent produced similar results. Smith and Dechant (1961), however, advocate that not more than one word in ten should be deleted when the cloze procedure is being used with children. The basis for the deletion of words may be structural or lexical and the nature of the blanks may be altered to provide additional cues for the reader: for example, first letters or upper-coastline cues could be retained (see Heatlie and Ramsey in press).

The advantages of Taylor's cloze procedure over conventional sentence completion exercises come from testing comprehension in a continuous prose passage instead of through a series of unrelated sentences. The cloze procedure measures the ability of a reader to use a variety of contextual interrelationships in completing any particular blank. It deals not only with specific word meanings but also the ability of the reader to respond to his own language pattern. It can be seen therefore that a response to a cloze test will reflect the total language abilities of the reader. In particular, it will reflect the way in which the reader can respond to cues using his combined primary and intermediate and higher reading skills in ways outlined by Merritt (1969b).

The value of the cloze procedure as a measure of readability has also been stressed by writers such as Bormuth (1963) and Rankin (1959) and Klare (1966) though there is disagreement on the possible extent of its valid use (e.g. Schlesinger 1968). Klare reports the criticism that words may be correctly restored to the passage on the basis of familiar patterns of expression while the passage remains only vaguely understood, i.e. using largely the primary and intermediate skills with little use of higher order skills. The use, by different authors, of different definitions of comprehension may account for this comment.

The possible use of the cloze procedure as a test of comprehension in evaluating readability formulae should not be overlooked. Bormuth (1963), in a study using the cloze procedure and multiple choice questions, concluded that the cloze tests were valid and consistent measures of reading comprehension and that they were superior to the multiple choice measures used in the study. He also concluded that the tests were appropriate for individuals differing widely in reading comprehension ability. It would seem that the cloze test may be best described as an index of, rather than a measure of comprehension.

A later research by Bormuth (1966) involved the use of the cloze test as a measure of comprehension in a detailed study of theoretical and practical problems in measuring readability. It is appropriate to outline the findings of this research since they provide a framework within which to discuss the value of the cloze procedure and the other measures of readability referred to in this part of the book.

Bormuth (1966) suggested that the present measures of readability could be considerably improved and that new and equally effective methods could also be devised. He reports a study in which he made a very thorough examination of new approaches to readability. He conducted an experiment in which twenty different passages in the form of a cloze test were given to groups of children in an elementary school in California. The scores on these tests were used as a measure of comprehension. Bormuth also analysed the passages, using a wide number of new and traditional linguistic factors. The results were discussed in relation to five major theoretical issues.

The first question which Bormuth considered was that of the linearity of relationship between difficulty of texts and reading ability. The results of his study of this question have already been discussed (page 98). The second question was whether the variables studied which influence difficulty for persons at one level of achievement have an equal influence on difficulty for persons at another level of achievement. Again, the findings on this question, which have already been referred to, suggest that a single readability formula can be used to predict difficulty for a wide range of reading abilities. This conclusion simplifies the problem for a teacher since, with judicious selection, one formula should cover the range of reading abilities in most groups of children.

The third question to be examined by Bormuth was whether it was possible to obtain useful formulae for assessing the readability of small language units. His conclusion was that the methods used could be regarded as useful but 'that the best possible linguistic variables for use on small language variables are far from being discovered.' The fact that Bormuth's results were inconclusive suggests that this aspect of readability could be examined further. Since children read a great number of short instructions, questions and so on, which are often found to be ambiguous, misleading and downright unreadable, teachers could gain a great deal of assistance in the control of the linguistic complexity of this kind of material if practical readability measures were developed.

Bormuth then considered the validity of readability formulae. He was particularly interested to find out whether the use of new linguistic variables and modern testing techniques could be used to improve readability formulae. To deal with this question, 47 variables (22 traditional and 25 form-class ratios) were correlated with one another. One conclusion was that available formulae contain too few variables. The main conclusion, however, was that the present level of precision of formulae could be markedly increased. In support of this conclusion, Bormuth points out that the variables which seem to be most useful are all newly developed.

The fifth question to be examined was whether techniques derived from the study of psycholinguistics and the computer translation of language are likely to be of use as new measures of readability. Bormuth's analysis of the data obtained on this question is very detailed but some general conclusions are drawn. Of the new factors measured, word depth, letter redundancy, form-class ratios, and letter counts were most promising. In particular, the simple exercise of counting the number of letters provided one of the best measures of the difficulty of words and also sentences.

At the present time, not all the findings and wealth of detail in this study have immediate practical application for a teacher, as yet. They do, however, indicate the ways in which readability research is likely to develop. Some conclusions and methods referred to, such as the value of letter counts, may be of immediate assistance in assessing readability even though the variable has not yet been incorporated into a simple and accurate formula. The report provides a wide perspective within which to evaluate current ideas on readability and has acted as a spur to reviving interest in the subject.

The discussion of various methods of assessing readability has shown that there is as yet no clearly established approach. Though some methods have been shown to have greater practical value than others, it is also evident that recent research is likely to produce results and methods which may be used by teachers to improve their effectiveness.

The cloze procedure seems to have a number of characteristics which should make it useful. As will be seen, it also has practical value in the teaching of reading. Two basic advantages of this procedure are, firstly, that it appears to reflect the sum total of all influences which interact to affect readability and so comes nearest to incorporating, in combination, the elements involved in the definitions of readability discussed earlier, and which formed the basis for so many techniques of measurement. Secondly, the performance of the reader is being measured on samples of the text to be read. Few other measures involve the juxtaposition of the intending reader and the text.

Up to this point, most of the methods of assessing readability have examined the two sides to be matched separately: for example, assessments of the reader are made using one set of criteria, such as knowledge of background, previous reading experience etc. Similar assessments, also subjective, are made of the book. Here, however, different criteria are adopted, such as format, impressions about illustrations etc. Thus, in addition to the unreliability of the subjective assessment, the match is rendered more unreliable through the use of different criteria to assess the reader and book. Objective assessments can, of course, be adopted, as we have already seen when reading age is assessed by a standardised reading test, and the book by the use of a formula. In this case, objectivity increases the reliability of the separate assessments but as the two sides of the match are still measured by reference to different criteria the gains may be less than one would wish. When the cloze test is applied, both reader and book

105

are assessed simultaneously by use of the one measure. This undoubtedly gives this procedure a greater face validity than other procedures referred to.

An attempt to incorporate the principle of the cloze procedure into a standard Reading Comprehension Test has been made recently by McLeod (1970). He has devised a simple test, entitled the GAP test, which is made up of two passages in which approximately every tenth word is deleted. McLeod does not delete every tenth word in sequence which means that there is variation in the number of words preceding the blanks. The two forms of the test, labelled B and R, are intended for use as alternatives. However, if greater precision is required, the two versions may be combined to provide an aggregate score. The tests are easy to administer and quick to score. Tables for converting scores into reading ages are provided for each form of the test and for the aggregate score of B and R.

This test does not involve the direct matching of reader and book which has been referred to in the use of the cloze procedure, since the reader is not tested on a sample of the material which he might read. This form of comprehension test does enable the teacher to measure the response to the different elements of language described earlier, in a way which is not possible using other techniques. The reading ages arrived at, using the GAP test, may be a better index of a child's ability to apply his reading skills than word recognition or established comprehension tests. An attempt to relate a reading age as measured by the GAP test and cloze measures of textual difficulty to a series of teachers' and children's estimates would provide the basis of a scale for predicting readability simply and reliably.

There is a problem, however, in linking two scores on different tests, even though they have a common basis, in that scores must be translated into the same scaled units and this presents rather severe methodological problems. Although there is as yet little evidence on which to judge the value of the test, there is good reason to expect that it will have value in a variety of clinical and teaching situations. A prepared battery of cloze passages of this type could provide quick yet accurate measures of the reading progress which have greater diagnostic and teaching value than many present procedures. In addition to the use of the cloze procedure, a number of informal uses can be suggested to assist in the assessment of readability.

Publishers and authors may find the procedure a sufficiently accurate and reliable test with which to assess readability levels of material prior to publication. For little cost and trouble, a number of cloze tests could be prepared using the material intended for publication as the sample. These tests would then be given to different groups of potential readers. The children would, of course, have to be of an appropriate age and their reading ability would have to be assessed independently on a standardised test in order to scale the cloze scores. In making these assessments, it would be preferable, for the reasons indicated earlier, to use a testing procedure which measures the same factors as those reflected in the readability measure. The results would give an indication of the extent to which the print is found to be readable. In this way, difficulties of expression, and other problems, may be more easily identified and controlled before publication. If a series of low scores on the cloze tests suggest that a passage is too difficult for the group for whom it is intended, then indices from readability formulae could be applied, in turn, to diagnose the difficulty. For example, if word length is short then there will probably be no problem at this level, but if the words are long, then a subjective evaluation of the long words would be useful. Similarly, if the sentence length is generally short, then there is probably no problem, but if sentences are long, then an examination of sentence complexity would be called for.

If word and sentence factors do not seem to be the cause of difficulty, then an examination of paragraph structure could be undertaken, and so on. At the highest level of difficulty causes of failure may be sought in the context of the passage, since the number of ideas or factual details (too few or too many) may be in need of modification. In this way, authors and editors would be modifying their work in a much more meaningful way than is usual, since amendments are being based upon the responses of a sample of the intended readership.

Again, if a small sample of text in the form of a cloze test was included in the front or back of the book, even as a separate pamphlet, for the children to complete, the publishers could give the teacher a quick and reliable means of assessing the suitability of reading material for the particular children for which it is intended. Given the present difficulties in selection of materials, this might prove of invaluable assistance to harassed teachers—a service which would be much appreciated and which, again, would seem to involve negligible cost. A practical advantage of this use of the cloze procedure which would make it very attractive to teachers is that it is easy to apply and involves little expertise of administrative 'know-how'.

Where a prepared cloze passage is not supplied by a publisher, the teacher could cannibalise one text and prepare some cloze passages by cutting out the appropriate words. The templates which would be prepared in this way would be re-usable since the children would write their responses onto a blank sheet lying beneath the passage. If this approach is not feasible because of the cost involved, then perhaps it would be worth ypting out samples from the texts, leaving spaces where appropriate. In this case, the children would be writing their responses on to a stencilled sheet. A collection of such sheets would provide teachers and children with a permanent record of reading success on texts of varying difficulty. The procedure is clearly simple enough for many children to apply and study themselves, and can provide the teacher with a variety of opportunities for advancing the children's fluency and comprehension in an efficient yet interesting manner.

In this way, cloze procedures could be applied to texts over which little or no control is exercised in selection, and would, if applied systematically, provide the readers with a means of judging the suitability of different materials for their level of attainment. In this way, too, the teacher could eventually classify all the books in the library corner in terms of their suitability for children with different levels of reading attainment. The use of a simple coding system would help the children in their selections by giving them clues about the difficulty of the language in addition to the information about the content, which they receive from reading the title, viewing illustrations etc. The arrangement of the books in this way would again involve the children in developing skills which they need to acquire in order to improve their reading.

SUMMARY

Various methods of assessing readability have been described and discussed. Many of the techniques referred to offer suitable means of dealing with the problem of matching a reader to a book. It is clear that methods of assessment may be improved by both revision and replacement of existing procedures and that current research indicates ways in which these improvements might be made.

When we come to practical matters, the study of readability seems to offer several possibilities, particularly to teachers. There is the value to the teacher in assisting with the problem of selecting suitable reading materials. Then, there is the possibility of using some techniques as teaching aids and also there is the possibility of children themselves using some techniques in order to evaluate their reading materials in their own way.

Readability also offers a profitable area of research in a variety of ways involving large scale and detailed studies, but also it offers a number of simple problems of the kind which can be undertaken by students in Colleges of Education, Institutes of Education and on other courses which require a review of the effectiveness of written communication, comprehension or reading difficulties. Indeed, there would seem to be an obvious need to extend the small amount of work on this subject which has already been undertaken in this country. To this end, the annotated bibliography is offered as a guide in the selection of suitable projects.

The intention of this study has been to introduce the reader to a systematic approach to a basic problem. It is hoped that it has provided a frame of reference with which to view this problem of selection and also the means to tackle the problem effectively. Above all, it is hoped that the study will have been found to be not only informative but also readable!

Selected Annotated Bibliography

This section contains selected references which may help a person wishing to read beyond the introductory information given in this monograph. Some references are included for the general background and review of research which they provide, others are included for the practical information which they contain and for their suitability as sources for further research, while others are included for the bibliographies and references which they provide. The list has been kept to a minimum with the intention of easing the reader's search for further reading, and the brief notes are given to help the reader to judge the relevance of the reference.

BORMUTH, J. R. (1966) 'Readability: a new approach.' *Reading Res. Quart.,* **1,** 79–132.

The author reviews the present position in the development of readability measures. Five major theoretical and practical problems are outlined. An experiment involving new and traditional readability measures was conducted to provide evidence on each of these issues. The sample used to test these factors was the population of one school in California. The subjects were divided into five form groups (135 subjects in each). The procedure for arriving at these groups is described. Intercorrelations between the difficulty of the passage and a wide range of variables, such as word frequency lists, word length, form class ratios and parts of speech ratios, are calculated and evaluated and several conclusions are drawn from these results. The detailed discussion is a valuable contribution to the study of readability and contains many ideas suitable for examination in small scale researches which might be easily undertaken. The article is essential reading for anyone studying readability seriously. The main conclusions are referred to in this monograph (see pages 104 to 105).

CHALL, J. S. (1958) *Readability: an appraisal of research and application.* Bureau of Education Res. Monographs No. 34. Ohio State University.

This is one of the few books in print devoted wholly to the study of readability. The main problems of assessing readability are outlined. Formulae in use up to the mid 1950s are collated, described and reviewed. A major section is devoted to the tabulation and discussion of empirical studies involving the various formulae. The application of readability studies to education is also considered and future lines of research are suggested. The book covers a wide range of factors which relate to the measurement of readability and contains general comment as well as detailed analysis. The book is likely to be useful for readers wishing to become more familiar with previous work on readability as well as for those who wish to study the topic of measurement more deeply than this monograph allows.

DALE, E. and CHALL, J. S. (1948) 'A Formula for Predicting Readability.' *Educ. Res. Bull.* 27 Jan. 11–20, and Feb. 37–54.

In the first part of this article, the authors discuss the shortcomings of previous formulae and describe the rationale of their own. The February edition of the bulletin contains detailed instructions for the application of their own formula. The article also includes the Dale-Chall 3000 word list, which represents words that are known by at least 80 per cent of children in Grade IV. This is an essential reference for readers who wish to experiment with the formula and it may also be helpful to other readers in view of its simple coverage of the major drawbacks of previous formulae and the clear statement of the rationale of the Dale-Chall formula.

DALE, E. and SEELS, B. (1966) *Readability and Reading: An annotated bibliography*. International Reading Association.

This bibliography contains a collection of articles from the period 1962–65. Only major sources prior to this period are referred to. There are nine sections covering many general aspects of readability as well as specific applications: general references, measuring, sentence structure, vocabulary, literary style, subject area materials, mass communications, literary materials and languages. A very useful source of references for teachers and students wishing to read chosen aspects of the subject. Use of this bibliography would save much time in finding relevant research.

ERIC/CRIER (LAFFEY ed.) (1967) *Recent Reviews and Bibliographic resources for Reading Research*. Indiana University.

This is a detailed collection of abstracts covering a wide range of researches into reading, many of which are concerned with readability. The aspects of readability included are too numerous to mention but each abstract contains sufficient detail to allow the reader to decide whether the reference is relevant to his purpose. This should be a very useful source of references for teachers and students in this country wishing to do research in reading. It is unfortunate that no similar storage and retrieval system exists in this country.

FILLENBAUM, S., JONES, L. V. and RAPOPORT, A. (1963) 'The predictability of words and their grammatical classes as a function of the rate of deletion from a speech transcript.' *J. of Verbal Learn. and V. Behav.*, **2,** 186–94.

The 'cloze' procedure is used to measure the predictability of various grammatical classes and verbatim responses in texts which have been mutilated in different ways. The technique used is adaptable for small scale research and the topic studied is of relevance to those interested in the problem of reading difficulty. The article is useful as an example of the application of cloze procedure.

The findings concerning the predictability of words and their class are relevant to the assessment of difficulty of reading materials and several conclusions are drawn which are of value to teachers, students and researchers into language.

FLESCH, R. F. (1948) 'A new readability yardstick.' *J. of App. Psychol.*, **32,** 221–33.

The author describes the rationale and method of use of one of the most popular readability formula. This is a modification of his earlier formula (1943). The reasons for modification are given. Details of the formula and comment upon it are now available elsewhere (see Chall 1958 and Klare 1963 in this text). Though still of use and easy to apply, it is doubtful whether teachers will find the formula as useful as other measures. The article is still valuable as an introduction to the measurement of readability through the use of formulae.

FRY, E. (1968) 'A readability formula that saves time.' *J. of Reading*, **11,** 513–16, 575–8.

The author gives directions for calculating his formula and using his readability graph. The simplicity in calculation and interpretation make it attractive to teachers. The graph is described but the expression of attainment in terms of reading grades diminishes its application in Britain. It could, however, be easily adapted for use in Britain. The article contains useful ideas for teachers or students wishing to undertake small scale research into the measurement of reading difficulty.

KLARE, G. R. (1963) *The Measurement of Readability*. Iowa State University Press.

This book contains a thorough examination of readability formulae. Practical applications and basic considerations in readability are outlined. The main part of the book is devoted to the description and discussion of the most common readability formulae, and to the discussion of their reliability and validity. The collection and description of formulae is particularly useful. The book assumes a certain amount of prior knowledge and is an academic discussion of the topic.

A detailed annotated bibliography is included. The references cover the use of formulae and reliability and validity studies undertaken over many years. While many references might seem out of date the annotations are sufficiently detailed to allow the reader to judge their relevance to his work. This book is essential reading for any person wishing to study readability formulae in detail. However, readers looking for information of more immediate practical value may find it less relevant.

MCLAUGHLIN, G. H. (1968) *Proposals for British Readability Measures.* Third International Reading Symposium (Eds: Brown, A. L. and Downing, J.) Cassell.

The author proposes a definition of readability, and outlines four main variables affecting readability; visibility, legibility, individual differences, and logical determinants. He then comments on linguistic factors which may be used to predict readability and describes models to explain word and sentence comprehension. Defects in present readability formulae are discussed and an alternative—readability tables—is proposed. This article contains suggestions involving large scale research for the preparation of these tables.

The article is a useful introduction to many ideas related to readability and is one of the few contributions by British writers to the literature on readability. It may be less useful to the reader who is familiar with the subject and is seeking more specific and detailed references.

MCLEOD, J. (1962) 'The Estimation of Readability of Books of Low Difficulty.' *Brit. J. educ. Psychol.,* **32,** 112–18.

The article describes two experiments carried out to assess the readability of elementary reading books. The results suggested that reliable readability levels could be obtained for each book.

In the first experiment 250 children were given a word recognition test and were then required to read extracts from the books. The readability of the books was calculated from the proportions of children at different reading levels who read extracts making not more than two mistakes. The second experiment used a measure of reading comprehension as the criterion, and readability levels were obtained which agreed substantially with the earlier results. Readability levels calculated using the Spache and Dolch formulae bore no clear relationship either to one another or the experimental findings.

The author concludes with a general discussion in which the potential of the 'cloze procedure' is considered. This article is useful as a reference for readers interested in the assessment of material for slow readers or children beginning to read, and for

113

readers wishing to follow up the idea of constructing readability tables.

MERRITT, J. E. (1970) *The Intermediate Skills: Towards a better understanding of the process of fluent reading.* Proceedings of the Sixth Annual Conference United Kingdom Reading Association, Ward Lock.

A thorough examination of the interrelationships between various skills found to influence fluency in reading. The author argues that there are a number of reading skills which lie outside the area of Primary Skills, which are essential to word recognition, but which are still below the level of 'Higher Order Skills', which are essential to comprehension. The skills which would be considered as 'intermediate' are described and exemplified, and their basis discussed. The way in which these skills affect the reading process is also described. Finally, the implications for teaching are considered and suggestions for activities to develop these skills are made.

The article is likely to increase a teacher's understanding of a number of reading skills which have received little attention and to lead to a more precise understanding of the function of different kinds of teaching procedures. The material it contains could also be useful to students learning about the teaching of reading.

SPENCER, H. (1969) *The visible word: problems of legibility.* Lund Humphreys (2nd Ed.)

A free ranging review of many aspects of legibility. The author does not confine his references and comments to conventional studies of legibility but covers in addition many aspects of modern technology and its effect upon the preparation and transmission of visual material. The author covers briefly a wide range of topics and also deals with explanations of some of the reported effects of legibility studies.

The author describes and comments upon methodology and results of research and summarises the conclusions on effects of type size, face, weight, case and angles of vision. A section is devoted to a consideration of old and new alphabets for print, including problems of computerisation and electronic transmission, all very clearly and fully illustrated with examples.

The author has included a glossary and comprehensive bibliography together with many ingenious and apposite illustrations and other visual displays of high quality. The book should be of interest not only to students of legibility and alphabet design but also to those involved in wider aspects of the study of reading because of its wide ranging comment and informative illustrations.

STRICKLAND, R. G. (1962) 'The Language of Elementary School Children: Its relationship to the language of reading textbooks and the quality of reading of selected children.' *Bulletin of the School of Education*. Indiana University, Vol. 38 4.

The author describes a system of analysis which was used to classify and describe children's language. Aspects of language, such as the syntactic structure of sentences, the frequency of occurrences of certain speech patterns, and the amount and kinds of subordination were investigated and related to characteristics of the children such as age, sex, intelligence and parental education. The book provides detailed information on the relationships uncovered and these aspects of the children's language are then compared to the language of chosen reading schemes.

The main value of this research lies in the evidence it has produced regarding patterns of language commonly used by children. The system of analysis is easy to understand and could be quickly adopted for further research. The other main value lies in the way discrepancies between the language used in books differs from the spoken language of children. This kind of study could be easily undertaken and would provide evidence which could be very helpful in construction of reading material for children of different ages. A very useful reference for teachers and students of reading as well as for those readers principally interested in readability.

TAYLOR, W. L. (1953) 'Cloze Procedure: A New Tool For Measuring Readability.' *Journalism Quarterly*, 415–33.

The author describes the principle involved in the construction of 'cloze' tests, how the method works and general theoretical considerations. Distinctions are drawn between this procedure and readability formulae and sentence completion tests. Two experiments are described which test the suitability of different kinds of deletions, the effect of marking synonyms as well as correct responses, and the effects of variation in order of presentation. The results of the experiments are used to evaluate the reliability and predictive value of the cloze test, the effect of variation in the form of presentation and the range of applicability of the tests. This article is an essential starting point for anyone wishing to use this technique as a measure of readability. It is also useful for readers concerned with the general theoretical considerations involved in measuring the difficulty of texts.

TINKER, M. (1965) *Bases for Effective Reading*. University of Minnesota Press.

This book summarises work conducted by the author over many years. It consists of five parts, each dealing with aspects of the perceptions and comprehension of print. Perception and reading, eye movements in reading, typography and reading, illumination and reading, and the appraisal of reading proficiency are each considered in turn. The author reviews the evidence on each aspect thoroughly and the book therefore serves as a useful source book for readers wishing to follow up the relationships between perception, legibility and readability.

This book contains paraphrases of parts of Tinker's earlier book *The Legibility of Print*. Readers wishing to follow up the more specific topic of legibility will find that *Legibility of Print* contains a more detailed treatment of the subject.

References

ABERNETHY, D., FERGUSON, S., MCKAY, Y. and THOMPSON, D. F. (1967) 'Children's in-school reading in Belfast—a suggestive survey.' *Reading*, **1**, 3.

BAYER, H. (1967) *Herbert Bayer: Visual Communication, Architecture, Painting.* New York: Van Nostrand-Reinhold.

BORMUTH, J. R. (1963) 'Cloze as a Measure of Readability' in *International Reading Association Conference Proceedings,* **8**, 131–4.

BORMUTH. J. R. (1966) 'Readability: a new approach.' *Reading Res. Quart.,* **1**, 79–132.

BROWN, R. and BELLUGI, U. (1964) 'Three Processes in the Child's Acquisition of Syntax.' *Harvard Educational Review,* **34**, 133–51.

BROWN, R. and BERKO, J. (1960) 'Word Association and the Acquisition of Grammar.' *Child Development,* **31**, 1–14.

CARROLL, J. B. (1964) *Language and Thought.* New York: Prentice-Hall.

CARTERETTE, E. C. and JONES, M. H. (1963) 'Redundancy in children's texts.' *Science,* **140**, 1309–11.

CHALL, J. S. (1958) *Readability: An appraisal of research and application.* Bureau of Educ. Research Monographs No. 34. Ohio State University.

CLARKE, M. (1970) in COX and WHITE (eds.) *Teaching Disadvantaged Children in the Infant School.* University College of Swansea: Department of Education.

DALE, E. and CHALL, J. S. (1948) 'A formula for predicting readability.' *Educ. Res. Bull.,* **27**, 11–20, 37–54.

DALE, E. and SEELS, B. (1966) *Readability and reading—An annotated bibliography.* Newark, Delaware: International Reading Association.

DOLCH, E. W. (1948) 'Grading Reading Difficulty' (Ch. XXI) in *Problems in Reading.* Champaign: The Garrard Press.

ENGLISH, H. B. and ENGLISH, A. C. (1958) *A Comprehensive Dictionary of Psychological and Psychoanalytical Terms.* London: Longmans.

EPSTEIN, W. (1961) 'The influence of syntactic structure on learning.' *Amer. J. Psychol.,* **74**, 80–85.

FILLENBAUM, S., JONES, L. V. and RAPOPORT, A. (1963) 'The predictability of words and their grammatical classes as a function of the rate of deletion from a speech transcript.' *J. of Verb. Learn. & Verb. Behav.*, **2**, 186–94.

FLESCH, R. F. (1948) 'A new readability yardstick.' *J. of app. Psychol.*, **32**, 221–33.

FRY, E. A. (1968) 'A readability formula that saves time.' *Journal of Reading II*, **7**, 513–16.

GIBSON, E. J., PICK, A., OSSER, H. and HAMMOND, M. (1962) 'The role of grapheme-phoneme correspondence in the perception of words.' *Amer. J. of Psychol.*, **75**, 554–70.

GIBSON, E. J., OSSER, H. and PICK, A. D. (1963) 'A Study of the Development of Grapheme-Phoneme Correspondences.' *J. of verb. Learn. and verb. Behav.*, **2**, 142–6.

GLANZER, M. (1962) 'Grammatical category: a rote learning and word association analysis.' *J. verb. Learn. and verb. Behav.*, **1**, 31–41.

GRAY, W. S. and LEARY, B. E. (1935) 'What makes a book readable: An initial study.' University of Chicago Press.

GUCKENHEIMER, S. M. (1947) 'The Readability of Pamphlets on International Relationships.' *Educ. Res. Bull.*, **26**, 231–8.

GUNNING, R. (1952) *The technique of clear writing*. New York: McGraw-Hill.

HEATLIE, S. and RAMSEY, E. (1971) 'An investigation into alternative methods of assessing the readability of books used in schools.' Proceedings of seventh Annual Study Conference of UKRA 1970. London: Ward Lock.

HUEY, E. B. (1908 and 1968) *The Psychology and Pedagogy of Reading*. New York: McMillan & Co. 1908 and M.I.T. Press 1968.'

KAMM, A. and TAYLOR, B. (1966) *Books and the Teacher*. London: University of London Press.

KLARE, G. R. (1963) *The measurement of readability*. Iowa: Iowa State University Press.

KLARE, G. R. (1966) 'Comments on Bormuth's readability: a new approach.' *Reading Research Quart.*, **1**, no. 4, 119–25.

KOLERS, P. A. (1968) 'The recognition of geometrically transformed text.' *Perception and Psychophysics*, **3**, 57–64.

KOLERS, P. A. (1969) 'Clues to a letter's recognition: Implications for the design of characters.' *Journal of Typographical Research*, **3**.

KOLERS, P. A. and PERKINS, D. N. (1969a) 'Orientation of letters and their speed of recognition.' *Perception and Psychophysics*, **5** (5), 265–9.

KOLERS, P. A. and PERKINS, D. N. (1969b) 'Orientation of letters and their speed of recognition.' *Perception and Psychophysics*, **5** (5), 275–80.

LAFFEY, J. (ed.) (1967) *Recent Reviews and Bibliographic Resources for Reading.* ERIC/CRIER system. Indiana University.

LOBAN, W. D. (1963) 'The Language of Elementary School Children.' in *N.C.T.E. Research Report,* No. 1. Champaign, Illinois: N.C.T.E.

LORGE, I. (1944) 'Word lists as a background for communication.' *Teachers College Record,* **45,** 543–52.

LUCKIESH, M. and MOSS, F. K. (1940) 'Boldness as a factor in type design and typography.' *J. appl. Psychol.,* **24,** 170–83.

MCLAUGHLIN, G. H. (1968) 'Proposals for British Readability measures.' *Third International Reading Symposium* eds. BROWN and DOWNING. London: Cassell.

MCLAUGHLIN, H. (1969) 'Smog Grading—a new readability formula.' *J. of Reading,* **22,** 639–46.

MCLEOD, J. (1962) 'The estimation of readability of books of low difficulty.' *Brit. J. Psychol.,* **32,** 112–18.

MCLEOD, J. (1970) *The GAP Reading Comprehension Test.* London: Heinemann Educational Books Ltd.

MCNALLY, J. and MURRAY W. (1962) *Key Words to Literacy.* London: Schoolmaster Publishing Co.

MERRITT, J. (1969a) 'Reading skills re-examined.' *Special Education,* **58,** 1.

MERRITT, J. E. (1969b) 'The Intermediate Skills: towards a better understanding of the process of fluent reading.' Proceedings of the 6th Annual Conference, United Kingdom Reading Association. London: Ward Lock.

MILLER, G. A. (1951) *Language and Communication.* New York: McGraw-Hill.

MORRIS, R. (1963) *Success and failure in learning to read.* London: Oldbourne.

MORRISS, E. C. and HALVERSON, D. (1938) 'Idea Analysis Technique.' Unpublished thesis: Columbia University Library.

MOYLE, D. (1971) 'Readability: the Use of Cloze Procedure.' Proceedings of the 7th Annual Study Conference, Durham 1970, United Kingdom Reading Association. London: Ward Lock.

MUGFORD, L. (1969) 'A new way of predicting readability.' *Reading,* **4,** (2), 31–5.

NILES, O. S. (1963) 'Comprehension Skills.' *The Reading Teacher,* **17,** 2–7.

PATERSON, D. G. and TINKER, M. A. (1940) *How to make type readable.* New York: Harper & Brothers.

RANKIN, E. F. (1959) 'The Cloze Procedure—its validity and utility.' Eighth Yearbook of the National Reading Conference, pp. 131–44, reprinted 1970 in *Measurement and Evaluation in Reading*

119

ed. FARR, R. New York: Harcourt Brace and World Inc.

REID, J. (1970) 'Sentence structure in reading.' *Res. in Educ.*, **3**, May, 23– 7.

RUDDELL, R. B. (1965) 'The Effect of Oral and Written Patterns of Language Structure on Reading Comprehension.' *The Reading Teacher*, **19**, 270–75.

SHAW, A. (1969) *Print for partial sight—a research report.* London: Library Association.

SCHLESINGER, I. M. (1968) Sentence Structure and the Reading Process. The Hague: Mouton.

SMITH, H. P. and DECHANT, E. V. (1961) *Psychology in Teaching Reading.* New York: Prentice-Hall International Inc.

SPACHE, G. (1953) 'A New Readability Formula for Primary Grade Reading Materials.' *Elementary School Journal,* **55**, 410–13.

SPENCER, H. (1969) *The Visible Word: problems of legibility.* London: Lund Humphries.

STRANG, R., and BRACKEN, D. K. (1957) *Making Better Readers.* Boston: D.C. Heath.

STRICKLAND, R. G. (1962) 'The language of elementary school children: Its relationship to the language of reading textbooks and the quality of reading of selected children.' *Bulletin of the School of Education,* Indiana University, **38**, 4.

TAYLOR, W. L. (1953) 'Cloze Procedure: a new tool for measuring readability.' *Journalism Quarterly,* **30**, 415–33.

THORNDIKE, E. L. and LORGE, I. (1944) *The Teachers' Word Book of 30 000 Words.* New York: Bureau of Publications, Teachers' College, Columbia Univ.

TINKER, M. A. (1963) *Legibility of Print.* Iowa State University Press.

TINKER, M. A. (1965) *Bases for Effective Reading.* University of Minnesota Press.

TINKER, M. A. (1966) 'Experimental studies in the Legibility of print: an annotated bibliography. *Reading Research Quarterly,* 1. 4. 67–118.

VERNON, M. D. (1929) *Studies in the Psychology of Reading.* (A. The errors made in reading.) London: H.M.Stationery Office, 5–26.

VERNON, M. D. (1957) *Backwardness in Reading.* Cambridge: Cambridge University Press.

WILLIAMSON H., (1966) *Methods of Book Design.* London: Oxford University Press.

YNGVE, H. V. (1960) 'A Model and an Hypothesis for Language Structure.' *Proceedings of the American Philosophical Society,* **104**, (5), 444–66.

ZIPF, G. K. (1935) *The Psycho-Biology of Language.* Boston: Houghton-Mifflin Co.

ZIPF, G. K. (1949) 'Human behaviour and the principle of least effort.' Cambridge, Mass: Addison-Wesley Press.

Index